COUNTRY HOST COOKBOOK

Gracious Traditional Recipes for Home Entertaining

BY RONA DEME

quick fox

Book design by Nina Clayton
Illustrations by Nava Atlas
Cover design by Burton Pollack
Front cover photography by Herbert Wise

Printed in the United States of America.
International Standard Book No: 0-8256-3172-6
Library of Congress Catalog Card No: 80-52715

In Great Britain: Book Sales Ltd., 78 Newman
             Street, London W1P 3LA.
In Canada: Gage Trade Publishing, P.O. Box
             5000, 164 Commander Blvd.,
             Agincourt, Ontario, M1S 3C7.

To my family past and present.

Contents

Foreword

Rona Deme's *Country Host Cookbook* is more than a cookbook. It is history and a beautifully painted picture of a full but simple life in England's Cheshire and in Cheshire, Connecticut. Food, its preparation, and its appreciation are in Rona's blood and under her skin. An accomplished pianist, she understands composition and appreciates variations in cooking similar to those in music; as she so rightly points out, the variations are "basically the same with extra notes."

Rona is one of the most sensitive women I know, loving the apple blossoms in her orchard in Connecticut and watching the tiny green apples grow into rosy fruit. Reluctant to cut down the old orchard, she plants young trees nearby and saves the old for the sheer beauty of the blossom, "windfalls" for butter, and the odd fallen branch for winter firewood.

The *Country Host Cookbook* is for cooks and noncooks. I can't think of any book I would rather have on my bedside table—with a reservation: if I open it during a sleepless hour, it creates a hunger that can only be satisfied by going to the kitchen and baking a scone or a cake.

Rona Deme has brought an English country kitchen to Lexington Avenue, New York City, and has provided those who cannot visit her Country Host shop with the next best thing: the recipes and lore to recreate the atmosphere in their own kitchens.

—MAURICE MOORE-BETTY

Acknowledgments

Special thanks to Maurice Moore-Betty for his encouragement; to Janet Malcolm, Mimi Sheraton, and others for writing about Country Host; to Rita Scott for saying "you should do a book"; to Margaret McFarlane, Jeanette Mall, Irene Sax, and John Tovey for their help, patience, and friendship. And finally, I want to thank all the friends and customers of Country Host who keep us on our toes.

Introduction

Someone in my Manhattan shop said to me a while ago, "You must write a cookbook and leave a heritage of Country Host recipes." Well, that made me feel special and I started writing down all the recipes I could remember from childhood.

I was born at my grandparent's house known as The Dairy, in the small village of Hampton in Cheshire, England. My Grannie Peters was a tiny woman given to cooking enormous quantities of food such as big roasts, lots of cheese, vegetables, rice puddings, and apple pies. Everyone came to the table at Grannie's and she would prepare extra quantities on weekends.

Grandad Peters would come in from the dairy and drink a tot of tea while washing his hands. He was a big man, 6 feet tall, with black hair, brown eyes, and a hearty appetite. His midday meal often consisted of rump steak sizzled in butter with lots of on-ions, oven-bottom bread and always a jug of ale. I remember watching Grannie cook the steak in a black iron frying pan on the open fire in the old kitchen. How she did it, I'll never know, but it tasted marvelous, and she only seasoned it with pepper and salt. I would sit on the big horsehair sofa along one side of the kitchen table and wait for Grandad to give me a bite of his steak and a sip of his beer.

My parents, my sister, and older brother lived just a little way from Grannie's. The Dairy was a special place to visit on Saturday mornings, because Grandad would give each of the children a silver threepence and a big chunk of milk ice from the pas-teurizer cooler.

As a schoolgirl, I loved to get on my bike on Saturdays and ride along with my twin aunts to the Bickerton Hills of Cheshire where we would pick whinberries (huckleberries). This was an all-day outing, and we took picnic lunches of Cheshire cheese, crusty bread, a jam tart or two, and most important of all, a flask of tea. After picking the berries we would start for home. At the bottom of the hill was a farmhouse where we would get a glass of milk straight from the cow to perk up our legs for the three-mile ride home.

My mother used to make the most wonderful whinberry jam, and she always said with such pride, "If it were not for the girls picking the berries, we'd never have this." I watched my Mam make jams, bottle fruits, and prepare pickles. I also learned from her how to make the lemon curd for little tarts. My father taught me how to plant shallots and how to weed them out, so later Mam could make her wonderful English pickles. Making pickles, especially pickled onions, was a long and tedious job, but there were always plenty of us to help.

My Grannie had big damson plum trees, and when September came, my uncles would climb the trees, shaking off the damsons for my sister and me to collect in big baskets. Grannie would share the fruit with my Mam and her other children, and the next day would be damson-jamming time.

Grandad kept a big garden, supplying the family with vegetables and selling the rest to other farmers. He also had lots of chickens that laid marvelous eggs and there were broody hens too.

As a surprise he occasionally took us to see the new chicks. Other farmers would trade him a brace of pheasant or partridge for the sausage Grandad made after he had slaughtered a pig. I

learned from him that the game birds had to hang in a cold pantry to "get high" or age.

On Sundays in September and October, we would hunt for chestnuts and walnuts. I remember making pickled walnuts, and roasting chestnuts in the ovens at the side of the fire grate, keeping the hot coals pushed towards the oven side. I would invariably get a tummyache from eating too many of them.

Mushrooms came into their own at this time of year too. I can still smell them cooking for ketchup. All of our preserving, bottling, and jamming was done on open coal fires.

For bottling fruit, Grannie used the same jars year after year. She washed and rinsed the jars and put them into the oven to dry and sterilize, although she never called it that. When the jars were very hot, she would take them out of the oven and fill each one with damsons, which she had already wiped with a cloth. She then poured sugar over the fruit, filling in all the spaces, and screwed on the lids. There was always a little room for expansion. The jars were placed back in the oven until the skins of the fruit cracked and the juices mixed with the sugar. When the sugar disappeared and a marvelous purple juice bubbled upwards, she pulled them out of the oven and let them cool on the kitchen table before putting them into the big pantry.

The pantry shelves were lined with all the fruits Grannie had bottled: gooseberries, greengage plums, black currants, whinberries, elderberries, raspberries, rhubarb, red currants, and many others. They never became

cloudy or moldy. She wasted nothing
and watching her put things up was a
sight to behold. We ate well then and
our pantries were well stocked, thanks
to the efforts and skills of the women
of the family. We did all of the baking,
roasting, and preserving in the same
oven, using just a few utensils. The
kitchen was the center of our house-
hold and the fireplace was the heart of
the kitchen. Because of these memories, making jams, jellies, and pickles is
still very special to me. I love to see
the sparkling reds and golds of the
fruits and vegetables sitting on the
shelves of the shop. Sometimes even
today, I would rather keep them to
look at than to sell them.

Christmas time was a joy and wonder.
In September Mam would begin baking
and putting together the plum puddings, Christmas cakes, and mincemeat.
She put the puddings in old white
bowls, wrapped the Christmas cake in
cheesecloth that was saturated from
time to time with brandy, and stored
it in an airtight tin. Woe betide anyone
who peeked inside. Everyone always
took a whiff of the cake before it was
wrapped up again after one of those
dousings. The mincemeat was kept in
a crock in a dark corner of the pantry.

We children could hardly wait for
Christmas to arrive. Four days before,
Mam would start baking and her little
mince pies would be gobbled up by
hungry relatives and friends. On Christmas Eve, we would hang our stockings
and leave a glass of sherry and a plate
of mince pies for Father Christmas.
The glass and empty plate would be
on view for us the next morning.
What excitement!

We always had two Christmas din-

ners—usually it was roast beef at our
home and roast goose at Grannie's.
The beef was served with Yorkshire
pudding, home-grown Brussels sprouts,
brown potatoes, mashed potatoes,
and runner beans. For dessert the
grownups feasted on plum pudding
with brandy sauce while we children
were served Bird's custard. Grannie
always made a marvelous sage stuffing for the goose as well as lots of
gravy and an onion-and-bread sauce.
At the end of these meals, the dirty
dishes were piled sky high, but we all
were there to help—no one was left
out.

New Year's meant a different kind of
meal—veal and ham pie with hard-
boiled eggs inside. It was so pretty
when it was cut showing flaky pastry,
pink ham, pale veal, and eggs. I learned
to bake this and other wonderfully
good things cooked by my mother
and my grannie.

After school there would be seed cake
and milk, Victoria sponge cake with
raspberry jam, or a chocolate Swiss roll
with whipped cream for special occasions. In February there was Shrove
Tuesday and Pancake Day:

Sole, Sole, Sole a cake
Please good missus a soleing cake
An apple or pear, plum or cherry
Anything good to make us merry.
The roads are dirty, my shoes are very thin,
I've got a little pocket to put a penny in.
If you haven't got a penny, a ha'penny will do,
If you haven't got a ha'penny, God bless you.

We went to all the homes in the village singing this song and receiving all
kinds of goodies, something like trick
or treat. Back at home Mam would
greet us with hot tea and cocoa and
thin pancakes that were rolled up and

sprinkled with sugar and lemon juice.

March and April brought spring, the time for gathering cowslips. Grandad gave us sixpence to collect big bunches of the fragrant wildflowers. He made a wine out of them, but we children never got to drink any.

There never was a more exciting time than gathering watercress from a brook that ran across the fields about a mile away from home. All of us knew exactly where and when to go and we would pull on our jerseys and wellingtons and rush off to get it. We had to wade into the shallow spring water to pick the watercress, but it was well worth it. Mam made the day special by baking currant scones. Watercress sandwiches on brown bread spread with sweet butter always tasted best when we had picked the greens ourselves.

In early August, Mam made a special supper with new potatoes that had just been dug out of the garden. She rubbed off the soil and put them into a pot of boiling salted water for about 25 minutes with several sprigs of mint, then drained and served them with gobs of butter. That was the main course on those nights, with scallions and radishes as a side dish—simple fare, but so good! Other favorite meals were suet puddings with treacle (molasses) or custard, Lancashire hotpot, leg of lamb with mint sauce, and roast beef with Yorkshire pudding and pickles. They were meals fit for a king, as my Grandad was wont to say.

Grandad used to take me to the market and that was the only time he bought any sweets. We loved hum-bugs—little pillows of hard candy with dark brown streaks that tasted like treacle, mint, and toffee all in one.

We often walked to the town of Malpas, two miles away, to see the fairs where Grandad's flowers were displayed and we could see horses jump. We carried picnic boxes filled with Cornish pasties, pork pies, and ginger beer. Church dinners were another big event and usually shepherd's pie was served, especially after the harvest festivals.

When I met the man who later became my husband, Frank was serving in the U.S. Army in England. By that time my family had moved to a town called Crewe. The war made us all appreciate the memories of plentiful food. We were on meager rations, especially sugar and butter. When our wedding day approached, relatives and friends donated their ration coupons to make a three-tiered wedding cake—we collected two ounces of butter here, some sugar there, raisins and mixed fruits everywhere, just as if we were gathering rare jewels. The cake was a tremendous success and everyone received a piece. No one thought of putting the cake under the pillow—it was too precious an item not to eat it.

During the war years we frequently had to use powdered eggs. We would either have a fresh egg and no bacon or the bacon and no powdered eggs, but we made do. Even now when I make a wedding cake for a customer of Country Host, I think how wonderful it is to have pounds of butter, the mixed fruits, and all the other makings of an English wedding cake at my fingertips.

When I came to America in 1946 I started a new life with new faces, new customs, and, of course, new food. My husband's parents were born in Hungary and they had come to America as young adults. I loved my mother-in-law—she spoke broken English, but she had her own way of expressing herself. Mama taught me a lot of her cooking secrets and her thrifty ways. I learned to make goulash, stuffed cabbage, chicken soup with dumplings, lekvar (prune butter), veal dishes, cookies, pies, and doughnuts. I've been very lucky to have good teachers. All these recipes were in my head and whenever my children wanted to make something they had to follow me around with pencil and paper to take down all the ingredients. I have always felt that recipes are like pieces of music—one learns the basic notes and then keeps practicing. Variations are just a few extra notes. I refer to some recipes as my light pieces and to some as my heavies. But I enjoy cooking to the fullest. Making pastry is just as enjoyable to me as picking watercress in the brook.

In 1946 my husband went into partnership in a pork store where they made their own sausages, smoked hams, salamis, and other pork products. Four years later we bought out his partner and undertook the business ourselves. I began to learn all sorts of new, exciting things such as cutting meat the proper way. We cooked every part of the pig—knuckles, feet, hams, pork chops, shoulders, and tenderloins. We made every type of sausage imaginable except bangers. This is an English sausage and it never occured to us that people here might like them. Ten years later my son

Peter began making bangers using his great-grandfather's recipe.

With a lot of hard work, we built a successful business. After my husband died I ran the shop alone for several years until the lease expired. Then I decided to do what was nearest my heart—open a food specialty shop. As children, my sister and I had always played shop. We called it Bebbington's and I was always the shopkeeper. On December 5, 1972, that dream was fulfilled when Country Host opened its doors.

Today my kitchens are very different from my mother's or grannie's. I have large bins of flour and sugar, electric mixers, and gigantic ovens. But I still use fresh eggs and butter for baking and I take pride in making our own bangers, meat pies, and fruit cakes. I feel proud when someone comes into the shop and says "Wow! It smells so good in here. What are you cooking? It reminds me of home many years ago."

I believe that cooking is a continual learning process. I am still learning, even after thirty years of business and a childhood that established the hows and whys of good things to eat. Food was always plentiful, simple, and good. This is my heritage and I have tried to put down the recipes as I remember them, with simple methods and good ingredients.

Soups

My in-laws taught me that soup plays an important role in the day's meals. I have carried on the tradition of making a soup almost every day for my family and Country Host. The bones from the ham we sell over the counter are invaluable and customers often ask for them to make their own soup or to use in flavoring a bean pot. Chicken soup is one of the most popular soups I make today—its healing powers are well known. Mama raised her own soup chickens and dressed them for the cook pot herself. These birds often contained the yolks of several unformed eggs that were a great delicacy in the soup. Fresh vegetables from the garden put into the simmering stock represent soup at its finest. I buy the best fresh chickens and vegetables that I can find to make my soup as much like Mama's as possible. In England soups still serve as main meals, especially in the farming districts. Known there as pottage, soup is served with pieces of bread to sop up the juices.

Chicken Soup

A 5-POUND CHICKEN, CUT INTO SERVING PIECES

3 TO 4 QUARTS WATER

6 CARROTS WITH GREENS, CHOPPED

1 BUNCH PARSLEY ROOTS WITH GREENS, CHOPPED

1 MEDIUM ONION, CHOPPED

1 GREEN PEPPER, CHOPPED

2 STALKS CELERY, CHOPPED

1 MEDIUM TOMATO, QUARTERED

1 KOHLRABI, CHOPPED

2 TABLESPOONS SALT

1 TABLESPOON WHOLE BLACK PEPPERCORNS

Place chicken (including the yellow fat and skin) into a large soup pot and cover with water. Bring to a boil, then turn down the heat. Cook gently for 1 hour. Skim two or three times to clarify. Add vegetables and seasonings. Cook over a low flame for 1½ hours more. Strain and serve with Liver Dumplings or homemade Egg Noodles (both on facing page).

10 TO 12 SERVINGS

Liver Dumplings

1 RAW CHICKEN LIVER,
FINELY CHOPPED

1 SMALL BUNCH PARSLEY,
FINELY CHOPPED

1 SMALL ONION,
GRATED

4 EGGS

½ TABLESPOON SALT

¼ TEASPOON BLACK PEPPER,
FRESHLY GROUND

2 CUPS FLOUR

Thoroughly mix ingredients together. If batter is too stiff, add a little water. Drop batter by the ½-teaspoonful into boiling salted water (1 tablespoon salt for every 2 quarts water). Cook about 15 to 20 minutes until the dumplings float. Remove with slotted spoon. Serve with fresh chicken soup.

Egg Noodles

3 EGGS,
LIGHTLY BEATEN

¾ CUP ALL-PURPOSE FLOUR

Mix eggs and enough flour to form a stiff dough. Knead on a floured board until smooth and elastic. Cover and let the dough rest for 10 minutes.

Roll out on a lightly floured board, until very thin. Let the dough dry for 10 minutes. Roll the sheet of dough into a tube and cut into thin strips with a sharp knife.

Cook the noodles in 2 quarts of boiling salted water, and serve with chicken soup. Or cook in chicken broth and serve as a side dish with a lump of butter instead of potatoes or rice.

Beef Soup

Add homemade Egg Noodles (page 9) to the soup, and you will have a hearty dish.

2 POUNDS SHIN BEEF OR CHUCK

1 SOUP BONE WITH MARROW

5 QUARTS COLD WATER

2½ TABLESPOONS SALT

½ TEASPOON BLACK PEPPER, FRESHLY GROUND

½ TEASPOON PAPRIKA

6 CARROTS

6 SPRIGS PARSLEY ROOTS AND GREEN TOPS

4 STALKS CELERY

2 MEDIUM ONIONS

2 MEDIUM POTATOES

Place meat and bones in a large soup pot. Cover with water and bring to a boil. Skim frequently. Add seasonings and simmer slowly for 1 hour.

Add carrots, parsley, celery, and onions. Cover and let simmer for 1½ hours.

Add potatoes and simmer for 1 more hour. Strain the soup and serve with pieces of the beef and vegetables.

10 TO 12 SERVINGS

Beef and Barley Soup

2 POUNDS SHIN BEEF IN ONE PIECE

10 CUPS BEEF STOCK (PAGE 201)

2 TABLESPOONS SALT

½ TEASPOON BLACK PEPPER

1 CUP BARLEY, SOAKED OVERNIGHT IN COLD WATER

8-OUNCE BAG DRIED GREEN PEAS

1 MEDIUM ONION, CHOPPED

2 LEEKS, CHOPPED

2 STALKS CELERY, CHOPPED

4 CARROTS, SLICED INTO ¼-INCH PIECES

1 SMALL TURNIP, PEELED AND DICED

2 MEDIUM POTATOES, PEELED AND QUARTERED

1 BUNCH PARSLEY, CHOPPED

Put the meat into a large pot with the stock, salt, pepper, barley, and peas. Bring to a boil and skim. Simmer for 1 hour. Add vegetables and simmer for 1½ hours. Remove meat from the soup and cut into small pieces. Return it to the soup. Heat again and serve with a sprinkle of parsley in each bowl.

10 TO 12 SERVINGS

Welsh Broth

Welsh and Scotch broths are made with lamb. I use shanks because the meat is less fatty. The Welsh border is about 5 miles from my birthplace, so we used many Welsh recipes. Welsh broth is a meal in itself—you can serve the broth first and have meat and vegetables as a separate dish.

5 LEEKS,
THINLY SLICED

4 LAMB SHANKS,
TRIMMED OF FAT

2½ QUARTS COLD WATER

1 TABLESPOON SALT

¼ TEASPOON BLACK PEPPER,
FRESHLY GROUND

5 CARROTS,
PEELED AND HALVED

1 SMALL TURNIP,
PEELED AND CHOPPED

5 MEDIUM POTATOES,
PEELED AND QUARTERED

1 TABLESPOON FLOUR MIXED TO A
SMOOTH PASTE WITH ¼ CUP WATER

3 TABLESPOONS PARSLEY,
CHOPPED

Chop the green part of the leeks and reserve.

Place shanks in a large soup pot, cover with water, add salt and pepper and bring to a boil. If necessary, skim the pot.

Add carrots, turnips, and white part of leeks. Cover and simmer for 2 hours, until meat is almost tender.

Add potatoes and cook slowly for another 30 minutes. Stir flour mixture into soup. Add the leek greens and parsley. Simmer for 10 minutes. Remove from heat and serve.

6 TO 8 SERVINGS

Scotch Broth

2 LARGE LAMB SHANKS,
TRIMMED OF FAT

2 QUARTS WATER

SALT AND PEPPER

2 TABLESPOONS PEARL BARLEY

2 SMALL WHITE TURNIPS,
DICED

2 MEDIUM CARROTS,
PEELED AND CHOPPED

1 LARGE ONION,
COARSELY CHOPPED

1 TABLESPOON PARSLEY,
CHOPPED

Put the shanks in a medium pot, add water and seasonings. Bring to a boil. Lower the heat and skim. Cover and simmer for 1 hour.

Add barley and continue cooking for another hour.

Add vegetables and simmer for 45 minutes, or until vegetables are tender.

Remove meat from pot and cut into small pieces. Return meat to soup and reheat. Serve sprinkled with parsley.

6 SERVINGS

Veal Vegetable Soup

This wonderful soup is so appetizing and appealing, I use it to begin any special meal.

1 POUND VEAL SHANK,
CUT IN 1-INCH CUBES

8½ CUPS WATER

1 TEASPOON SALT

4 CARROTS,
SLICED INTO ¼-INCH PIECES

1 CUP FRESH OR FROZEN PEAS

1 TABLESPOON BUTTER

1 TABLESPOON FLOUR

1 SMALL ONION,
CHOPPED

Place veal in a soup pot, add 8 cups of water and salt. Cook slowly for 1 hour. Add carrots and cook until tender. Add peas and cook gently for 10 to 15 minutes.

In a small saucepan, melt butter and blend in flour. Brown slightly and add onion and ½ cup water. Bring to a boil, stirring constantly. Add this mixture to the soup, stirring vigorously and bring back to the boil before serving.

6 SERVINGS

Farina Dumpling Soup

This takes a little extra preparation, but it is worth the effort.

1 ONION,
FINELY CHOPPED

4 TABLESPOONS SWEET BUTTER

1 POUND VEAL,
CUT INTO 1-INCH CUBES

1½ TABLESPOONS SALT

1/8 TEASPOON FRESHLY GROUND
BLACK PEPPER

3 CARROTS,
DICED

1 KOHLRABI,
DICED

2 LARGE POTATOES,
DICED

1 MEDIUM ONION

2 QUARTS WATER

3 SPRIGS PARSLEY ROOTS
WITH GREENS

FARINA DUMPLINGS
(RECIPE FOLLOWS)

In a large pot, brown onion in butter. Add veal and seasonings. Cover and simmer for about 40 minutes, adding a little water if necessary. Add vegetables and water. Tie parsley sprigs together and add to soup. Cook gently for 45 minutes, or until vegetables are tender. Remove parsley.

Drop farina dumplings into soup by the teaspoonful and simmer another 15 minutes.

6 SERVINGS

Farina Dumplings

1 EGG,
SEPARATED

½ CUP FARINA

¼ TEASPOON SALT

Beat egg white until stiff, then fold in slightly beaten egg yolk. Season with salt. Slowly add farina to egg to form a stiff dough.

Split Pea Soup

This thick soup is a great favorite. In England it is served with a splash of malt vinegar. In America, I serve it with a spoonful of sour cream or croutons.

1 LARGE HAM BONE,
CUT INTO 3 OR 4 PIECES

3 QUARTS WATER

1 BAG DRIED SPLIT GREEN PEAS

2 MEDIUM CARROTS

2 STALKS CELERY

1 POTATO,
PEELED

In a large pot, cover ham bones with water. Bring to a boil, stirring once or twice. Add vegetables and return to a boil. Lower the heat, cover and simmer for 2 hours. Remove bones from the soup and strain. Mash the vegetables through a food mill into the soup. Stir and season to taste.

6 TO 8 SERVINGS

Cabbage Tomato Soup

1 SMALL HEAD CABBAGE,
GRATED

1½ TEASPOONS SALT

2 TABLESPOONS FLOUR

1 CUP SOUR CREAM

1 CUP FRESH TOMATO JUICE

FRESHLY GROUND PEPPER

Place cabbage and salt in a medium pot with enough water to cover. Cook until tender. Mix flour and sour cream together. Add the tomato juice, and pour this mixture into the cabbage. Bring to a boil, stirring well. Serve hot with a twist of black pepper.

6 SERVINGS

Creamed String Bean Soup

A favorite in the summertime, served cold.

1 POUND FRESH STRING BEANS,
CUT IN ½-INCH PIECES

2 QUARTS WATER

1 TABLESPOON SALT

4 TABLESPOONS FLOUR

3 CUPS MILK

1 CUP SOUR CREAM

¼ CUP CIDER VINEGAR

Cook beans in salted water until tender—do not overcook. Drain.

Mix flour with enough water to make a smooth paste. Blend with sour cream and milk. Place beans in a medium saucepan, then cover with cream mixture. Add vinegar. Let soup come to a boil, stirring well. Serve hot with pieces of toast or chill.

8 SERVINGS

Leek and Potato Soup

This is soothing for an upset tummy.

6 LEEKS,
CUT INTO 1-INCH PIECES

6 LARGE POTATOES,
PEELED AND QUARTERED

3 QUARTS CHICKEN STOCK (PAGE 201)

SALT AND PEPPER

2 OUNCES BUTTER

Place vegetables in a large pot and add chicken stock. Bring to a boil. Lower heat, cover, and simmer for 2 hours. Put vegetables and liquid through a food mill. Stir and season to taste. Add butter, stir and serve.

6 TO 8 SERVINGS

Lettuce Soup

This heralds summer. I make it from my own garden lettuce.

1 LARGE HEAD LETTUCE

1 TABLESPOON SWEET BUTTER

6 SCALLIONS,
CHOPPED

1 CUP CHICKEN STOCK (PAGE 201)

1 CUP MILK

1 CUP HEAVY CREAM

SALT AND PEPPER

¼ TEASPOON GRATED NUTMEG

Wash and dry lettuce, then tear into large pieces. Melt butter in a deep frying pan, add scallions, and cook gently until soft. Add lettuce, cover and cook for 5 minutes.

Add chicken stock and milk. Cover and simmer for 20 minutes. Cool and purée in a blender or food processor. Just before serving reheat gently and season to taste. Add cream. Heat through but do not boil. Serve with a sprinkling of nutmeg.

4 TO 6 SERVINGS

Cream of Broccoli Soup

1 LARGE BUNCH BROCCOLI

2 TABLESPOONS SWEET BUTTER

1 TABLESPOON ONION,
CHOPPED

3 STALKS CELERY,
CHOPPED

4 TABLESPOONS ALL-PURPOSE FLOUR

4 CUPS CHICKEN STOCK (PAGE 201)

2 CUPS HOT MILK

SALT AND PEPPER

NUTMEG

Cook broccoli until tender. Drain and reserve the water. Reserving 2 large stalks, chop broccoli into tiny sprigs. Put stalks through a sieve or purée in food processor. Reserve.

Melt butter in a medium saucepan. Add onion and celery. Cook until tender, then stir in flour. Cook for 3 to 4 minutes. Slowly stir in chicken stock. Stir until nearly boiling, then add broccoli purée and milk. Strain soup into another saucepan. Add broccoli sprigs. Bring to the boil, stirring often. Remove from heat and season with salt and pepper. Sprinkle with nutmeg.

6 SERVINGS

Tripe Soup

This soup is well-known in the North Midlands of England. My Grandad Peters loved to eat cold honeycomb tripe with pepper and salt and a "lashing" of malt vinegar.

1 POUND PREPARED HONEYCOMB TRIPE,
CUT INTO 3 x ½-INCH STRIPS

2 CUPS WATER

1 CUP ONIONS,
CHOPPED

4 TABLESPOONS SWEET BUTTER

4 TABLESPOONS FLOUR

2 CUPS MILK

SALT AND PEPPER

CHOPPED PARSLEY

Place tripe in a medium saucepan with water and onions. Cook slowly for 45 to 50 minutes.

In another medium pot, melt butter. Add flour, stirring vigorously for 4 to 5 minutes. Gradually add milk, stirring constantly. Remove from heat and add cooked tripe and onions to the white sauce. Blend well. Season to taste with salt and pepper. Heat before serving and garnish each bowl of soup with a sprinkle of parsley.

8 SERVINGS

Parsnip Soup

Parsnips are popular in England and often are used as a side dish for roast meats. Cooked like carrots and served with lots of butter, they have a taste all their own.

3 CUPS PARSNIPS,
CHOPPED

1 TABLESPOON SWEET BUTTER

½ CUP ONIONS,
CHOPPED

¼ CUP CELERY,
CHOPPED

6 CUPS CHICKEN STOCK (PAGE 201)

2 TABLESPOONS CORNSTARCH

2 CUPS MILK

SALT AND PEPPER

¼ CUP FRESH LEMON JUICE

Melt butter in a large pot, add vegetables, cover and cook for 10 minutes. Do not brown. Add chicken stock and simmer gently for 40 minutes, or until the vegetables are tender. Purée the vegetables and stock in a food mill or blender. Reheat.

Mix cornstarch with milk and stir into the soup. Reheat, stirring often. Add salt and pepper to taste. Add lemon juice and stir. Serve with toast squares.

8 TO 10 SERVINGS

Watercress Soup

3 LARGE BUNCHES WATERCRESS

½ CUP SWEET BUTTER

½ CUP ONIONS,
CHOPPED

2 CUPS CELERY LEAVES,
CHOPPED

8 TABLESPOONS ALL-PURPOSE FLOUR

6 CUPS MILK

6 CUPS CHICKEN STOCK (PAGE 201)

SALT AND PEPPER

1 CUP HEAVY CREAM

Blanch watercress, reserving a few leaves for garnish. Finely chop the remainder. Melt butter in a large pot. Add watercress, celery leaves, and onions. Cover and cook for 5 minutes. Stir in flour. Remove from heat.

Gradually stir in milk and stock. Simmer for 15 minutes.

Pour soup through a strainer. Reheat and season with salt and pepper. Remove from heat and blend in the cream. Garnish with watercress leaves.

8 TO 10 SERVINGS

Notes

Potted Meats, Pâtés, Croquettes, Fritters, Savory Pies, and Puddings

In the days before refrigeration, preserving fish and meats was essential. Fish was salted and smoked, and pork was salted in brine for days, then smoked. Beef was salted and boiled or salted and dried. Potting gave variety to the monotonous diet of salted meats. Cooked fish or meat was ground or pounded into a paste-like consistency, seasoned with herbs such as thyme, cloves, pepper, salt, and a lacing of brandy and then packed tightly into earthenware pots. The pots were sealed with melted butter or fat and stored in cool pantries. Today potted meats are made and served on the same principle as pâté and terrines. Clarified butter is used to seal mixtures that can be kept stored in the refrigerator for several weeks if seal is unbroken.

Potted meats are excellent to have on hand for toast or tiny sandwiches or to serve an unexpected guest or as a starter to a meal. Some potted meats or pâtés must be pressed while cooling to solidify the finished product. I usually put a plate on top of the cooling dish, and set a quart container full of water on the plate for weight.

Potted Beef

2 POUNDS BONELESS SIRLOIN BEEF

1 CUP BEEF STOCK

6 CLOVES

½ TEASPOON ANCHOVY SAUCE

SALT AND PEPPER

6 OUNCES CLARIFIED BUTTER
(PAGE 189)

Place all ingredients in casserole dish, cover and bake in a 325°F. oven for 2½ hours. The meat will be very tender and falling apart. Discard cloves. Strain liquid and set aside. Put meat through the fine blade of a meat chopper 2 or 3 times or use blender or food processor. Mix to a smooth paste. Add half of the clarified butter and 2 or 3 tablespoons of cooking liquid. The consistency should resemble stiffly whipped cream. Taste for salt. Put the paste in ramekins or a large deep dish. Cool, then cover with remaining clarified butter and refrigerate. Serve with toast.

8 SERVINGS

Potted Chicken

1½ POUNDS COOKED CHICKEN

½ POUND LIGHTLY SALTED BUTTER

¼ TEASPOON GROUND MACE

¼ TEASPOON NUTMEG

¼ TEASPOON BLACK PEPPER

3 TABLESPOONS COGNAC

4 OUNCES CLARIFIED BUTTER
(PAGE 189)

Put chicken through the fine blade of a food chopper or food processor. Blend chicken and butter together. Add seasonings and mix thoroughly. Place mixture in potting dish. Spoon brandy over mixture. Cover completely with clarified butter. Refrigerate until cold. Serve with toast.

6 SERVINGS

Potted Ham

1½ POUNDS LEAN SMOKED HAM

½ POUND FRESH PORK FATBACK

¼ TEASPOON GROUND MACE

¼ TEASPOON NUTMEG

¼ TEASPOON BLACK PEPPER

1 CUP CHICKEN STOCK

2 TABLESPOONS COGNAC

4 OUNCES CLARIFIED BUTTER
(PAGE 189)

Put ham and pork fat through food chopper twice. Add spices and chicken stock. Blend well. Place mixture in a covered casserole dish and bake in a 325°F. oven for 2 hours. Cool, then strain off liquid and reserve.

Pound meat mixture to a smooth paste. Add cognac and enough of the cooking liquid to give a soft consistency. Taste for seasoning. If ham is mildly cured, some salt may be necessary. Spoon mixture into a serving dish and cover mixture with clarified butter. Refrigerate until set.

6 SERVINGS

Potted Calf's Liver

3 STRIPS BACON

1¼ POUNDS CALF'S LIVER

1 MEDIUM ONION,
FINELY CHOPPED

1 SMALL CLOVE GARLIC,
CRUSHED

10 TABLESPOONS BURGUNDY WINE

5 TABLESPOONS HEAVY CREAM

¼ TEASPOON BLACK PEPPER,
FRESHLY GROUND

¼ TEASPOON BASIL

SALT

2 OUNCES CLARIFIED BUTTER
(PAGE 189)

Fry bacon until crisp, then drain. Reserve the fat. Wipe liver and remove any sinew or gristle. Fry liver, onion, and garlic in bacon fat for about 10 minutes—do not overcook. Remove from pan and put through food chopper twice. Set aside.

Add wine to the pan and reduce by half. Cool.

Mix liver with cream and reduced wine. Season with pepper, basil, and salt. Crumble bacon into small pieces and add to mixture. Put in ramekins and press until cold. Cover with clarified butter. Refrigerate. Serve with toast.

6 SERVINGS

Potted Kipper Pâté

3 LARGE COOKED SMOKED
KIPPER FILLETS

6 OUNCES BUTTER

1/8 TEASPOON BLACK PEPPER,
FRESHLY GROUND

JUICE OF ½ LEMON

PARSLEY SPRIGS

LEMON SLICES

Remove any skin and bones from fillets. Blend fish, butter, and pepper into a smooth paste. Mix in lemon juice. Spoon the pâté into a 4-cup mold and chill. Before serving, garnish with parsley and lemon slices. Serve with toast.

6 SERVINGS

Country Pâté

8 SLICES FRESH PORK FATBACK

2 OUNCES BUTTER

1 OUNCE CORNSTARCH

½ CUP MILK

1 POUND CALF'S LIVER

1 EGG,
BEATEN

4 TABLESPOONS CREAM OR
3 TABLESPOONS CREAM WITH
1 TABLESPOON COGNAC

¼ TEASPOON BLACK PEPPER,
FRESHLY GROUND

1 TEASPOON SALT

¼ TEASPOON BOUQUET GARNI

Butter a loaf pan and line the bottom and sides with 5 slices of the fatback. Trim the slices to fit. Heat butter in a pan, stir in cornstarch and cook for 4 to 5 minutes. Gradually add milk, stirring constantly to prevent lumps. Return to the boil, cooking until thick and smooth. Remove from heat and set aside.

Grind liver and remaining fatback through a food chopper once or twice until the texture is smooth. Add liver, egg, and cream to sauce. Mix thoroughly. Add pepper, salt, and bouquet garni and mix again. Spoon mixture into loaf pan. Cover with aluminum foil, tucking carefully on all sides. Place loaf pan in a large pan filled with cold water. Cook for 45 to 50 minutes in the center of a 350°F. oven. Cool. Cover and press with weight. Refrigerate until ready to use.

6 SERVINGS

Chicken Liver Pâté

2 POUNDS FRESH CHICKEN LIVERS

4 OUNCES RENDERED CHICKEN FAT

2 MEDIUM ONIONS,
CHOPPED

4 OUNCES SWEET BUTTER OR
CHICKEN FAT

1 TEASPOON CELERY SEED

1 TEASPOON SALT

¼ TEASPOON BLACK PEPPER

2 TABLESPOONS GIN

Rinse and dry chicken livers. Melt chicken fat in a deep heavy pan. Add chicken livers and 1 onion, then cook for 15 minutes over a medium heat. Remove from heat and set aside.

Melt butter (or chicken fat) in another frying pan and sauté remaining onion until golden brown.

Put chicken livers and onion through food chopper. Put onion and butter liquid through food chopper, then add to chicken livers, mixing well. Add seasonings and adjust salt to taste. Add gin and mix thoroughly. Spoon mixture into a large bowl or 10 to 12 small containers for individual servings. Decorate with capers and olives. Use as spread for crackers or crusty French bread.

8 SERVINGS

Jellied Chicken Mold

A 3- TO 4-POUND BOILING CHICKEN

2 PIG'S FEET,
WASHED AND SCRUBBED

2 TEASPOONS SALT

¼ TEASPOON BLACK PEPPER

1 SMALL BUNCH BOUQUET GARNI
(THYME, BASIL, AND TARRAGON)

WATER

2 HARD-BOILED EGGS,
SLICED

Place chicken in large pot with pig's feet, salt, pepper and bouquet garni. Cover with cold water and bring to a boil. Cover pot, place in a 300°F. oven, and cook for 4 hours. Remove bouquet garni, strain stock and reserve. Let meat cool. Remove meat from chicken and pig's feet. Chop finely. Return meat to strained broth and heat through. Sprinkle a little water in a one-quart mold and line with eggs. Slowly pour meat mixture over eggs. Let cool, then press with a weight. Refrigerate overnight. Turn mold onto a bed of crispy lettuce and serve with cucumbers in vinegar and wholewheat bread.

4 TO 6 SERVINGS

Chicken Croquettes

2 CUPS COOKED CHICKEN
(1 LARGE CHICKEN BREAST)

1 TEASPOON ONION,
FINELY CHOPPED

1 TEASPOON PARSLEY,
CHOPPED

1 TEASPOON LEMON JUICE

½ TEASPOON SALT

¼ TEASPOON BLACK PEPPER

2 TABLESPOONS BUTTER

½ CUP ALL-PURPOSE FLOUR

1 CUP HALF-AND-HALF

1 OR 2 EGGS,
LIGHTLY BEATEN

BREAD CRUMBS

VEGETABLE OIL FOR FRYING

Combine chicken, onion, parsley, lemon juice, salt, and pepper.

Make a white sauce: Melt butter in a heavy saucepan, add flour, mix and cook over a low heat for 8 to 10 minutes; add half-and-half, stirring until sauce thickens. Add chicken, mix thoroughly, and cool. Shape mixture into 6 or 8 cylinders. Dip each croquette into crumbs, then egg and then crumbs again. Refrigerate for several hours. The croquettes are easier to handle when cold.

Heat vegetable oil to 340°F. and fry until golden brown. Remove with slotted spoon and drain on paper towels.

6 TO 8 SERVINGS

Cheese Croquettes

3 TABLESPOONS BUTTER

3 TABLESPOONS ALL-PURPOSE FLOUR

2/3 CUP MILK

2 EGG YOLKS

½ CUP GRUYÈRE CHEESE,
GRATED

1 CUP CHEDDAR CHEESE,
CUBED

¼ TEASPOON PAPRIKA

SALT

1 EGG,
LIGHTLY BEATEN

BREAD CRUMBS

VEGETABLE OIL FOR FRYING

Melt butter, stir in flour, and cook over low heat for 5 minutes. Add milk, stirring well until sauce thickens. Stir Gruyère into sauce. As soon as this melts, add Cheddar cheese, paprika, and salt to taste. Pour into a well-greased pan to cool.

When cool, cut into strips or circles. Dip each piece into crumbs, then beaten egg, then crumbs again. Heat oil to 340°F. and fry until golden brown. Drain on paper towels.

4 SERVINGS

Ham Croquettes

2 CUPS MASHED POTATOES

1 TABLESPOON BUTTER

3 EGG YOLKS

1/8 TEASPOON CAYENNE PEPPER

1 CUP COOKED SMOKED HAM,
CHOPPED

1 EGG,
LIGHTLY BEATEN

BREAD CRUMBS

VEGETABLE OIL FOR FRYING

Beat mashed potatoes, butter, 2 egg yolks, and cayenne pepper until smooth. Refrigerate.

Mix ham with remaining egg yolk and warm over low heat to cook slightly. Cool mixture.

Shape a tablespoon of potato mixture into a ball. Make a hole in the ball with finger. Place a teaspoonful of ham mixture in the hole, then shape back into a ball. Roll in crumbs, then in egg and again in crumbs. Continue until ingredients are used. Fry until golden brown in oil heated to 340°F. Remove with slotted spoon. Drain on paper towels.

4 SERVINGS

Salmon Croquettes

2 TABLESPOONS BUTTER

1/3 CUP FLOUR

1 CUP HALF-AND-HALF

½ TEASPOON SALT

1/8 TEASPOON BLACK PEPPER

1/8 TEASPOON CAYENNE PEPPER

2 CUPS FRESH OR CANNED SALMON,
FLAKED

1 TEASPOON FRESH LEMON JUICE

1 EGG,
LIGHTLY BEATEN

BREAD CRUMBS

VEGETABLE OIL FOR FRYING

Melt butter in heavy saucepan, add flour and cook over low heat for 5 minutes. Add half-and-half, stirring well until sauce thickens. Add seasonings, salmon, and lemon juice. Spread mixture in a shallow dish. When thoroughly cooled, shape into balls or cylinders. Roll in bread crumbs, then egg and then in bread crumbs again. Heat oil to 340°F., then fry croquettes until golden brown. Remove with slotted spoon and drain.

4 SERVINGS

Corn Fritters

2 CUPS FRESH OR CANNED CORN

1 TEASPOON SALT

1/8 TEASPOON PEPPER

1 EGG,
WELL BEATEN

1 TEASPOON MELTED BUTTER

½ CUP MILK

2 CUPS ALL-PURPOSE FLOUR

1 TEASPOON BAKING POWDER

VEGETABLE OIL FOR FRYING

Chop corn very finely or put through food chopper. Add seasonings, egg, butter, milk, flour, and baking powder. Mix well. Drop tablespoonfuls into deep oil heated to 340°F. and fry until golden brown. Remove with slotted spoon and drain. Serve with applesauce.

YIELD: ABOUT 30 FRITTERS

Clam Fritters

2 CUPS FLOUR

1 TEASPOON BAKING POWDER

½ TEASPOON SALT

1 CUP MILK

½ CUP CLAM JUICE

2 EGGS

24 SOFT CLAMS,
CHOPPED

SALT AND PEPPER

Make a batter by mixing flour, baking powder, salt, milk, clam juice, and eggs. Season clams with salt and pepper, then add to batter mixture. Drop tablespoonfuls into oil heated to 340°F. and fry until golden brown. Remove with slotted spoon and drain. Serve with fresh lemon slices and Tartar Sauce (page 47).

YIELD: ABOUT 36 FRITTERS

Sweetbreads and Oyster Pie

1 PAIR PREPARED SWEETBREADS
(PAGE 80)

2 DOZEN OYSTERS,
CLEANED AND SHUCKED

1 TABLESPOON BUTTER

1 TABLESPOON FLOUR

1 CUP HEAVY CREAM

2 EGG YOLKS,
HARD BOILED AND FINELY CHOPPED

SALT AND PEPPER

1 REGULAR SHORTCRUST PASTRY
(PAGE 195)

1 EGG,
LIGHTLY BEATEN

Break sweetbreads into small pieces. Melt butter in a medium-sized saucepan over a medium heat, mix in flour and cook for 5 minutes. Gradually add cream, stirring constantly to prevent lumping, and cook until sauce thickens. Add egg yolks, sweetbreads, and oysters. Mix together and season to taste. Put in a deep baking dish and cover top with pastry. Make two slits in top. Brush with beaten egg. Bake in a 375°F. oven for 45 to 50 minutes, until pastry is golden brown.

4 SERVINGS

Onion Pie

½ REGULAR SHORTCRUST PASTRY
(PAGE 195)

2 TABLESPOONS BUTTER

1½ POUNDS LARGE SPANISH ONIONS,
THINLY SLICED

3 EGGS

1 CUP MILK

SALT AND PEPPER

Prepare the pastry.

Melt 2 tablespoons butter in a heavy saucepan. Add onions, cover and cook until soft.

Beat eggs with milk, season to taste. Add the onions to milk mixture and pour into the pastry shell.

Bake in a 425°F. oven for 35 to 40 minutes until the pastry is golden brown and the filling is set and browned.

6 SERVINGS

Cornish Pasties

1 REGULAR SHORTCRUST PASTRY
(PAGE 195)

1 POUND TOP ROUND STEAK,
CUT INTO SMALL PIECES OR CHOPPED

1 LARGE ONION,
CHOPPED

4 MEDIUM POTATOES,
DICED

1 CARROT,
DICED (OPTIONAL)

SALT AND PEPPER

1 EGG,
LIGHTLY BEATEN

Prepare the pastry.

Mix meat, vegetables, and seasonings. Divide into 6 portions. Roll out the dough to a ¼-inch thickness. Cut into six 6-inch circles. Place a portion of filling on half of each circle. Brush edges with water. Bring opposite side of circle over the top of the filling and seal edges by pressing with the tines of a fork. Place on a baking sheet and brush tops with egg wash. Bake in a preheated 400°F. oven for 20 to 25 minutes, or until well browned.

NOTE: Puff pastry circles can be used for these Cornish pasties. Parboil the potatoes and carrot, chop, and combine with onions and meat and proceed with the recipe.

YIELD: 6 PASTIES

Savory Ducks

This old recipe is also known as faggots and poor man's goose. These are very popular for high tea.

1½ POUNDS PORK LIVER,
WASHED, DRIED

2 LARGE ONIONS

4 OUNCES BREAD CRUMBS

3 OUNCES BEEF SUET,
CHOPPED

2 TEASPOONS FRESH SAGE,
CHOPPED

2 TEASPOONS SALT

¼ TEASPOON BLACK PEPPER

½ CUP BOILING WATER

Grind liver and onions through fine blade of food chopper. Mix with bread crumbs, suet, salt, pepper, and sage. Mix thoroughly.

Form into balls the size of eggs. Place closely side by side in a baking pan. Bake in a 350°F. oven for 35 to 40 minutes.

Pour water into pan and scrape residue to form gravy when cooking time is through.

4 TO 6 SERVINGS

Scotch Eggs

6 HARD-BOILED EGGS

6 TABLESPOONS SAUSAGE MEAT

FLOUR

1 EGG,
LIGHTLY BEATEN

BREAD CRUMBS

VEGETABLE OIL FOR FRYING

Roll each hard-boiled egg in flour. Wet hands and shape a thin layer of sausage meat around floured egg. Roll in beaten egg, then in bread crumbs. Press bread crumbs gently so that excess does not spill off into oil. Place in 1½ to 2 inches oil heated to 350°F. Brown egg on one side 2 or 3 minutes, and then on the other side 2 or 3 minutes, or until egg is golden brown all over. Remove with slotted spoon to dish with paper towels to drain.

4 TO 6 SERVINGS

Savory Sausage Bake

2 OUNCES LARD

1 POUND SLICED BACON,
CUT INTO SMALL PIECES

2 MEDIUM ONIONS,
CHOPPED

3 MEDIUM TOMATOES,
SKINNED AND CHOPPED

4 OUNCES FRESH BREAD CRUMBS

2 OUNCES OATMEAL

SALT AND PEPPER

2 EGGS,
LIGHTLY BEATEN

3 TABLESPOONS MILK

2 POUNDS SAUSAGE MEAT
(RECIPE FOLLOWS)

Melt lard in a heavy skillet and saute onions and bacon over low heat for 4 minutes. Add tomatoes and cook for 1 minute longer. Remove from heat and mix in bread crumbs, oatmeal, salt, and pepper. Combine eggs and milk and stir this into mixture. Spoon mixture into a greased shallow baking dish. Arrange sausage patties on top.

Bake in a 350°F. oven for 35 to 40 minutes, or until sausage is cooked. Serve with applesauce.

6 TO 8 SERVINGS

Sausage Meat

1¾ POUNDS BONELESS FRESH
PORK SHOULDER

6 OUNCES STALE BREAD CRUMBS

1 TEASPOON SALT

¼ TEASPOON BLACK PEPPER,
FRESHLY GROUND

1 TEASPOON SAGE

Grind pork through meat chopper twice. Soak bread crumbs in cold water for 5 minutes, then squeeze out the water and add to sausage meat. Add salt, pepper, and sage and mix well. Form into 8 patties.

Toad-in-the-Hole

A favorite recipe.

8 BANGERS (ENGLISH SAUSAGES)

YORKSHIRE PUDDING BATTER
(RECIPE FOLLOWS)

8 WALNUT-SIZED KNOBS OF
BEEF DRIPPINGS

Put bangers into baking dish. Cook for
about 10 minutes in a 450°F. oven.
Pour off liquid from sausages. Add
beef drippings and return to oven for
5 minutes. Pour Yorkshire Pudding
over the bangers and return to oven
for about 30 minutes. Check after 20
minutes, and if the batter is browning
too quickly, lower heat to 425°F.

4 SERVINGS

Yorkshire Pudding Batter

2 CUPS ALL-PURPOSE FLOUR

PINCH OF SALT

2 EGGS

2 CUPS MILK OR 1½ CUPS MILK AND
½ CUP ICED WATER FOR
LIGHTER BATTER

Sieve flour and salt together into a
bowl. Add eggs and beat mixture well.
Gradually beat in just enough liquid
to make a stiff, smooth batter. Let
stand for a few minutes, then whisk in
the rest of the liquid.

Bubble and Squeak

Usually made with leftover potatoes and cabbage.

1 POUND MASHED POTATOES

1 POUND COOKED CABBAGE, CHOPPED

SALT AND PEPPER

BACON FAT

Mix mashed potatoes and cabbage together until smooth. Shape into a flat cake. Heat bacon drippings in a frying pan, and brown the cake on both sides. Serve hot with leftover meats.

4 SERVINGS

Colcannon

3 LARGE LEEKS, WASHED AND FINELY CHOPPED

2 TABLESPOONS BUTTER

½ CUP HEAVY CREAM

1 POUND MASHED POTATOES

1 POUND COOKED CABBAGE, CHOPPED

SALT AND PEPPER

Sauté leeks in 1 tablespoon of butter until soft. Stir cream into leeks. Mix potatoes, cabbage, and leeks together. Salt and pepper to taste. Shape into a flat cake and fry in remaining butter until brown on both sides. Serve hot with cold meats.

NOTE: You can add a cup of mashed turnips or leftover carrots to the mixture.

4 SERVINGS

Quiche

1 REGULAR SHORTCRUST PASTRY
(PAGE 195)

12 TABLESPOONS SWISS OR
JARLSBERG CHEESE,
GRATED

6 TABLESPOONS HAM,
CHOPPED, OR
6 TABLESPOONS COOKED SPINACH

3 TEASPOONS ONION,
CHOPPED

2 EGGS

SALT AND PEPPER

½ CUP HEAVY CREAM

½ CUP MILK

1 TABLESPOON CORNSTARCH

NUTMEG

Prepare the pastry. Roll out to fit 4-
or 5-inch quiche dishes or a 9-inch pan.

Cover the bottom of each pastry shell
with 1 tablespoon cheese. Add 1 tablespoon of ham or spinach. Sprinkle
each portion with ½ teaspoon onion.
Sprinkle with remaining cheese.

Combine the eggs, salt and pepper,
cream, and milk. Mix well. Add cornstarch and whisk. Pour custard mixture
over the shells. Sprinkle with nutmeg
and bake in a 375°F. oven for 40 to
45 minutes, or until golden brown.

YIELD: 6 TO 8 4-INCH QUICHES OR A
9-INCH QUICHE

Cheese Pudding

4 THICK SLICES WHITE BREAD,
TRIMMED

BUTTER

8 OUNCES SHARP CHEDDAR CHEESE

½ TEASPOON DRY MUSTARD

2 DASHES EACH OF BLACK PEPPER,
CAYENNE PEPPER, AND NUTMEG

1 EGG,
LIGHTLY BEATEN

1 CUP MILK

1 CUP CREAM

Toast bread on one side and butter
the untoasted side. Place two slices,
toasted side down, in a greased casserole dish. Sprinkle with half of the
cheese and seasonings. Repeat, using
remaining toast and cheese.

Bring milk and cream to the boil. Add
remaining seasonings. Pour the hot
milk-cream mixture over egg. Pour
over the toast-cheese mixture. Let
stand for 30 minutes to let toast soak
up the liquid. Place in a 350°F. oven
until pudding rises and is light brown.

2 SERVINGS

Welsh Rarebit

1 TABLESPOON MILK

3 OUNCES SHARP CHEDDAR CHEESE,
GRATED

1 EGG YOLK,
LIGHTLY BEATEN

SALT AND PEPPER

DASH OF WORCESTERSHIRE SAUCE

1 PIECE TOAST,
BUTTERED

Slowly melt milk and cheese in small saucepan. Add egg yolk and seasonings, stirring until thickened. Pour over buttered toast. Garnish with sliced tomato and watercress.

1 SERVING

Soufflé of Stilton Cheese

3 TABLESPOONS BUTTER

2 TABLESPOONS PLAIN FLOUR

1/8 TEASPOON EACH SALT AND PEPPER

½ TEASPOON DRY MUSTARD

4 OUNCES STILTON CHEESE,
CRUMBLED

1 CUP MILK

3 LARGE EGGS,
SEPARATED

Melt butter in a heavy saucepan. Add flour, salt, pepper, mustard, cheese, and milk. Stir constantly over low heat until sauce comes to a boil and thickens. Remove from heat. Beat egg yolks lightly and add 2 or 3 tablespoons of the hot cheese mixture to the yolks and stir together. Stir egg yolk mixture into hot cheese mixture. Beat egg whites until stiff, then carefully fold into the cheese mixture. Blend well. Spoon the mixture into a buttered 2-pint soufflé dish. Cook in preheated 400°F. oven for 35 to 40 minutes, or until soufflé puffs nicely. Serve with fresh spinach salad and crusty French bread.

2 TO 3 SERVINGS

Haggis

Haggis is a form of savory pudding. The mixture for haggis traditionally fills a sheep stomach, but here is a haggis that is steamed in a pudding basin and served with the usual accompaniment of mashed potatoes and turnips.

8 OUNCES SHEEP LIVER

4 OUNCES BEEF SUET

2 MEDIUM ONIONS,
PARBOILED

4 OUNCES OATMEAL

SALT AND PEPPER

Rinse the liver. Place in a medium-sized pot, cover with cold water, bring to a boil, and simmer for 35 minutes. Drain and reserve the liquid. Grind liver through the fine blade of a food chopper. Grind onions and beef suet through the chopper (put the suet through before the onions). Combine liver, suet, and onions.

Brown oatmeal in a heavy skillet over medium heat for a few minutes. Add oatmeal, salt, and pepper to liver mixture. Mix well. Moisten mixture with liquid from boiled liver, using just enough to form a soft dropping consistency. Put mixture into a 2-pint greased pudding bowl. Cover with 2 sheets of greased waxed paper. Tie paper on securely and steam for 2 hours. Check once or twice that enough water is in steamer. Serve hot with mashed potatoes and turnips.

4 SERVINGS

Fish

Be very careful when buying fish to see that it is really fresh. It should have firm flesh, bright eyes, and a mild smell—fresh fish does not smell offensive. Buy fish as close to the time of cooking as possible. If it is purchased several hours before using, store the fish at the top of the refrigerator as near to the freezer as possible until ready for cooking. Fish should be cooked quickly. Poach, broil, fry or bake in foil for best results. Not too long ago fish was a cheaper buy than meat. Today, fish is not at all inexpensive and some fish prices are as high as meat. An excellent source of protein and quick to cook, fish makes a light but substantial main course.

In my home years ago our fish dishes consisted mostly of fresh cod, halibut, gray sole, lemon sole, fresh haddock, and smoked haddock (more commonly known as Finnan haddock). There were special times when we had salmon and fresh trout. Our annual seaside holidays meant fish and chips wrapped in newspaper. Sometimes we would sit in a cafe and have that special treat along with smacks and green peas, all liberally coated with malt vinegar and shakings of pepper and salt. Smacks are slices of huge potatoes, coated with the same batter as the fish and deep fried.

I also associate those seaside holidays with cockles, mussels, and oysters. The stalls had huge displays of shellfish near steaming cook pots, and the proprietors tempted everyone, shouting, "Come and get your cockles and mussels," "Oysters for sale," "Fresh oysters," "Fish, fish, beautiful fish."

I can still hear it all, and smell the ocean and feel the ocean waves banging against the sea wall, splashing our faces.

Fish and Chips

Fillet of sole is excellent for this dish, although any fresh white fish fillet will do.

8 PIECES WHITE FISH FILLET,
ABOUT 4 INCHES LONG

1 CUP FLOUR

1 TEASPOON SALT

BATTER
(RECIPE FOLLOWS)

VEGETABLE OIL

4 POTATOES,
PEELED AND SLICED INTO FRIES

MALT VINEGAR

SALT AND PEPPER

LEMON WEDGES

Wash and dry the fish well. Mix flour and salt together in a shallow dish. Dip each piece of fish into the flour, shaking off excess. Dip each floured piece into the batter, allowing excess batter to drip off.

Heat 1½ to 2 inches vegetable oil in heavy skillet to 340°F. Do not allow fat to get too hot. Brown fish about 5 minutes on one side, then turn and brown the pieces on the other side for another 5 minutes—do not overcook. Drain on paper towels.

Fry potato chips to accompany fish. Sprinkle with malt vinegar and seasonings if desired. Serve with lemon wedges.

4 SERVINGS

Batter

1 CUP ALL-PURPOSE FLOUR

PINCH OF SALT

2 EGGS

½ CUP MILK

Sift flour and salt into a bowl. Add eggs and mix well. Add ¼ cup milk and mix to a stiff dough. Let stand for a few minutes. Gradually add remaining milk and beat to a smooth batter. Let batter rest in refrigerator for about 1 hour. Give a final whisk before using. If any batter is left over after battering fish, use it to dip ¼-inch slices of potato to make smacks. Or leftover batter can be poured into a lightly greased pan to make a big fat pancake.

Finnan Haddock Poached in Milk

Finnan Haddock gets its name from the fishing village of Findon, Kincardineshire, Scotland, where the curing and smoking of haddock was introduced. The fish is salted and hung in chimneys to smoke over peat fires.

1½ POUNDS SMOKED HADDOCK

3 TABLESPOONS BUTTER

3 CUPS MILK

BLACK PEPPER,
FRESHLY GROUND

3 EGGS

Wipe haddock pieces with a damp cloth. Melt butter in a heavy skillet. Add haddock and enough milk to almost cover the fish. Twist fresh black pepper onto each piece of fish. Bring milk to a boil and lower heat. Simmer gently for 15 to 20 minutes. Remove fish from skillet to an oven-proof dish. Keep warm until served.

In the remaining liquid, poach the eggs for 2 minutes, keeping heat at a simmer. Serve a poached egg on top of each piece of haddock.

3 SERVINGS

Haddock Balls

1½ POUNDS FINNAN HADDOCK,
POACHED IN MILK
(RECIPE THIS PAGE)

¼ TEASPOON BLACK PEPPER,
FRESHLY GROUND

1½ TABLESPOONS PARSLEY,
CHOPPED

½ POUND MASHED POTATOES

2 EGGS,
BEATEN

BREAD CRUMBS

VEGETABLE OIL FOR FRYING

Chop fish as finely as possible. Add pepper, parsley, and mashed potatoes. Mix thoroughly and shape into 8 balls. Dip balls into eggs, then coat with bread crumbs. Heat 1½ to 2 inches vegetable oil in heavy skillet to 350°F. Brown fish balls in oil 3 to 5 minutes. Drain on paper towels. Serve hot or cold with sliced tomatoes and watercress.

4 SERVINGS

Kedegree

1 POUND FINNAN HADDOCK,
POACHED IN MILK (PAGE 42)

2 HARD-BOILED EGGS

2 CUPS COOKED LONG-GRAINED RICE

1/8 TEASPOON CAYENNE PEPPER

1 CUP CHEDDAR CHEESE,
GRATED

CHOPPED PARSLEY

LEMON WEDGES

Flake the haddock coarsley with a
fork, removing any bones. Remove
yolks from eggs and chop the whites.
Add to haddock. Mix in rice and cayenne pepper. Heat this mixture in a
saucepan over a low flame, stirring once
or twice with a fork. Stir in cheese. Remove from heat and place on a hot
serving dish. Sprinkle with sieved egg
yolks and parsley. Garnish with lemon
wedges and serve immediately.

NOTE: Cheese can be omitted and a
white sauce (page 92) served on the
side.

4 SERVINGS

Baked Halibut Steaks

2 POUNDS HALIBUT STEAK

2 TABLESPOONS BUTTER

1 CUP MILK

SALT AND PEPPER

Butter both sides of the fish. Lightly
salt and pepper each side. Place fish
steaks flat in a baking pan and add the
milk. Bake in a 350°F. oven for 35 to
40 minutes, basting fish several times
until the milk is used up.

4 SERVINGS

Baked Cod Fillets with Bacon Stuffing

4 OUNCES BACON,
CUT INTO SMALL PIECES

¼ CUP ONIONS,
CHOPPED

½ CUP MUSHROOMS,
CHOPPED

3 TABLESPOONS BUTTER

½ CUP FRESH BREAD CRUMBS

1½ CUPS MILK

SALT AND PEPPER

2 COD FILLETS, ABOUT 1 POUND EACH

1 CUP CHEDDAR CHEESE,
GRATED

2 TABLESPOONS ALL-PURPOSE FLOUR

2 TOMATOES,
SLICED

CHOPPED PARSLEY

In a heavy skillet, fry bacon, onions, and mushrooms until tender. Add 1 tablespoon of butter. Stir in bread crumbs and a little milk to mix. Season with salt and pepper.

Wipe fish with damp paper towels. Remove skin. Place one fillet in a baking dish and cover with the bacon stuffing. Place other cod fillet on top of stuffing.

In a saucepan, melt remaining butter with milk. Add flour and ¾ cup cheese. Heat, stirring continuously until sauce thickens. Season with salt and pepper. Pour sauce over the fillets. Arrange sliced tomatoes on top of sauce and sprinkle with remaining cheese. Bake for 45 to 50 minutes in a 350°F. oven. Sprinkle with chopped parsley.

4 SERVINGS

Baked Perch with Cream Sauce

A simply done fish, but tasty and colorful.

8 PERCH WITHOUT HEADS

8 OUNCES PLAIN YOGURT

¼ CUP HEAVY CREAM

SALT AND PEPPER

LEMON SLICES

TOMATO SLICES

PARSLEY SPRIGS

Wash fish thoroughly and pat dry with paper towels. Place side by side, alternating placement of heads and tails, in a shallow baking dish. Season with salt and pepper. Mix the yogurt and heavy cream together and pour mixture over the fish. Bake, uncovered, in a 375°F. oven for 35 minutes, or until fish flakes easily with a fork.

Garnish with lemon and tomato slices and parsley sprigs.

4 SERVINGS

Fish Pie

JUICE OF 1 LEMON

1 POUND COD FILLETS OR
FRESH SALMON

2 TABLESPOONS BUTTER

SALT AND PEPPER

2 TABLESPOONS FLOUR

½ CUP MILK

¼ POUND FRESH OR FROZEN
GREEN PEAS

2 CUPS MASHED POTATOES (CREAM
WITH LOTS OF MILK AND BUTTER)

GRATED NUTMEG

Squeeze lemon juice over fish. Wrap fish in foil with 1 tablespoon butter and season to taste. Steam over a pan of boiling water for 15 to 20 minutes.

Place remaining butter, flour and milk in a saucepan and cook over low heat until sauce thickens. Remove bones and skin from steamed fish. Flake the fish and fold into the sauce. Taste for seasonings. Fold in green peas. Put fish mixture into medium-sized baking dish. Cover with creamed potatoes. Sprinkle with nutmeg. Heat through before serving.

4 SERVINGS

Haddock Curry

2 POUNDS HADDOCK FILLETS

½ CUP ONIONS,
CHOPPED

1 SMALL CLOVE GARLIC,
FINELY CHOPPED

3 TABLESPOONS BUTTER

1 SMALL APPLE,
PEELED, CORED, AND CHOPPED

2 CLOVES

1 TABLESPOON CURRY POWDER

2 TABLESPOONS ALL-PURPOSE FLOUR

1 CUP MILK

1 CUP CHICKEN STOCK

2 MEDIUM TOMATOES,
PEELED AND CHOPPED

¼ CUP RAISINS

2 TEASPOONS TOMATO PURÉE

2 TABLESPOONS CHUTNEY

1 PIECE FRESH GINGER,
CHOPPED

SALT AND PEPPER

LEMON WEDGES

Remove skin from haddock and cut into 1-inch cubes. Sauté onion and garlic in butter over a low flame for about 5 minutes. Add apple and cloves and cook a few minutes more. Stir in curry powder, then add flour and cook another 5 minutes.

Remove from heat and stir in milk and stock. Stirring constantly, bring to a gentle boil, lower heat, and continue cooking until mixture thickens. Add tomatoes, raisins, purée, chutney, ginger, and salt and pepper. Cover pan and cook slowly for 10 minutes. Stir in fish and cook 10 to 15 minutes, or until fish is tender. Do not overcook.

Serve over cooked rice with lemon wedges on the side.

6 SERVINGS

Fillet of Sole with Tartar Sauce

1 POUND FILLET OF SOLE,
CUT INTO 2-INCH STRIPS

½ CUP ALL-PURPOSE FLOUR,
SEASONED WITH 1 TEASPOON SALT
AND 1/8 TEASPOON PEPPER

1 EGG,
BEATEN

BREAD CRUMBS

1 CUP VEGETABLE OR PEANUT OIL
FOR FRYING

LEMON SLICES

Coat fish strips in seasoned flour, then coat each strip with egg and bread crumbs. Let these pieces sit for a few minutes.

Prepare Tartar Sauce (recipe follows).

Heat oil in heavy skillet. Fry fish until golden brown, about 2 to 3 minutes on each side. Do not overcook. Put the browned fish pieces onto a heated platter.

Garnish with lemon slices and serve with tartar sauce.

4 SERVINGS

Tartar Sauce

1 HEAPING TEASPOON CAPERS,
FINELY CHOPPED

1 HEAPING TEASPOON CORNICHONS,
FINELY CHOPPED

1 HEAPING TEASPOON ONION,
FINELY CHOPPED

1 HEAPING TEASPOON PARSLEY,
FINELY CHOPPED

¼ CUP THICK MAYONNAISE

1 TABLESPOON HEAVY CREAM

Mix all ingredients together and refrigerate until ready to use.

Salmon Steaks

2 8-OUNCE SALMON STEAKS

SALT

2 TEASPOONS BUTTER

2 TEASPOONS LEMON JUICE

2 SPRIGS DILL

1 TEASPOON VEGETABLE OIL

Wipe salmon with damp paper towels. Sprinkle each piece with salt, 1 teaspoon butter, 1 teaspoon lemon juice and a sprig of dill. Place each steak in aluminum foil, carefully folding the ends to make as waterproof as possible.

Put wrapped fish packets into a heavy pot and cover with cold water and add 1 teaspoon salt and vegetable oil to water. Bring water slowly to a boil.

If serving the fish cold, remove pot from heat when the water boils. Set aside with fish packets remaining in the water. This keeps the fish moist. When water is cool, unwrap each packet carefully and place on a serving dish. Refrigerate before serving. Garnish with watercress, tomatoes, and lemon slices.

If serving hot, lower heat when water comes to a boil and simmer for 7 minutes. Remove salmon packets from water, unwrap and place on a heated platter. Serve with buttered fresh green peas, cooked in a little salted water with a sprig of fresh mint, and boiled new potatoes with parsley butter (recipe follows).

2 SERVINGS

Parsley Butter

3 TABLESPOONS BUTTER

2 TEASPOONS LEMON JUICE

1 TABLESPOON PARSLEY, CHOPPED

½ TEASPOON SALT

1/8 TEASPOON PEPPER

Cream butter. Add lemon juice, parsley, salt, and pepper. Mix well. While potatoes are still hot, add parsley butter and mix to distribute over the boiled new potatoes.

Mussel Stew

This can be made with cockles, clams or scallops.

3 QUARTS (ABOUT 60-80) MUSSELS,
WELL SCRUBBED

WATER TO COVER

2 TABLESPOONS BUTTER

1 LARGE ONION,
SLICED

1 CLOVE GARLIC,
CRUSHED

½ POUND MUSHROOMS,
FINELY CHOPPED

½ CUP BREAD CRUMBS

1 TABLESPOON LEMON JUICE

1 TABLESPOON PARSLEY,
CHOPPED

4 TABLESPOONS SHERRY

SALT AND PEPPER

1 EGG YOLK

4 TABLESPOONS HEAVY CREAM

Place mussels and water in a large cooking pot, cover, and bring to a boil. Reduce heat and cook gently for about 5 minutes until shells are open. Drain and reserve the liquid. Remove mussels from shells.

Melt butter in a heavy skillet. Cook onion and garlic for 3 minutes, then lightly sauté mushrooms. Add bread crumbs, lemon juice, mussel liquid, parsley and sherry. Mix well, then season to taste. Bring mixture to a boil, turn down heat and simmer for 5 minutes. Combine egg yolk and cream. Add to mussels, but do not boil.

8 SERVINGS

Meats

When I came to America in 1946 the first weekend was spent in Connecticut at my inlaws' farmhouse. I can still smell the scent of the big old lilac trees that surrounded Mama's summer kitchen and the aroma coming from the enamel coffeepot perking away on the woodstove. The farm was very old and at one time had been the site of the first shoe manufacturing concern in Connecticut. My first meal was chicken paprikas. Never having tasted such food in England and not having had rich foods for a long time because of the war, I was not too happy eating it—in fact, I thought it was awful. Of course, I would not have said anything for the world; they were doing their best to make me feel welcome. Eventually I learned how to make this dish from Mama, and learned to love eating it too.

Satisfying dishes that bring out the best flavor of meats and fish; simple hearty food—that sums up traditional British cooking and most other traditional cooking as well. This was also true of the recipes my mother-in-law brought from Hungary—delectable and thrifty dishes. Foods are used in season and vegetables treated with loving hands. The first carrots to come from the garden, the first peas and string beans, ripe tomatoes—all had a special place in Mama's dishes. Corn was very special. When I was a child corn was bought by Grandad to feed the chickens: I was surprised to learn that the first ears of corn to ripen at the Connecticut farm were picked and cooked in huge pots of salted boiling water and served as a big treat. Lumps of farm butter were rubbed up and

down the ears of corn and before long my taste buds were enjoying every kernel. Ripe tomatoes were searched for and we usually ate them as a side dish with corn. I learned to can tomatoes from my mother-in-law.

Traditional Hungarian food was served in abundance on weekends when relatives visited Mama and Papa. Sometimes as many as twenty aunts, uncles and cousins would arrive at the farm. My husband Frank and I had our business in New York City in those days but we spent most weekends in Connecticut, much as my family and I do today. On those visiting weekends, we would bring Frank's sausages, such as kolbasz and hürke. When the weather was good we had a picnic at the farm.

Kolbasz is a delicious smoked sausage made of freshly ground pork, seasoned with salt, paprika, and mashed garlic. This mixture is stuffed into a thin casing, twisted into 12-inch sausages, and placed in the smokehouse for 48 hours. At those picnics the kolbasz was cut into 3- or 4-inch pieces, then held on a stick over the outdoor fire to brown and cook just like a frankfurter or pieces would be added to pots of Mama's stuffed cabbage.

Hürke is a meal in itself. It is made of cooked, ground pork liver and hearts, seasoned with marjoram, mixed with fried onions and cooked rice, then stuffed into sausage skins about 8 inches long and lightly smoked. This most satisfying sausage is real country food—fried in a pan to crisp the outside skin and then eaten.

Our smokehouse was filled with these sausages. They were strung up like big bunches of bananas, then hung on smoke-sticks in the smokehouse. We used hickory and oak chips for smoking, and the smell from our smokehouse was enjoyed by our customers as well as by Frank and me.

There are not many licensed smokehouses in New York City anymore. Rising costs have been a factor, and, as I know firsthand, it is blooming hard work.

Another important part of the picnic would be the roasting of salt pork over the open fire. This is the white back fat of the pork, sometimes seasoned in a brine of garlic and salt or left plain. My father-in-law would cut up the pieces of fat into 2- or 3-inch lengths and spear them onto long apple sticks made from the wild apple shoots from the base of the trees. Because they were freshly cut and full of sap, these sticks would not burn as quickly over the fire. The fat was held over the fire and would begin to melt. These drippings were allowed to drop onto pieces of rye bread topped with a slice of onion. As the fat became smaller, the bread and onion soaked up the drippings. By the time the fat became a delicious brown crackling, one ate the bread and onion with gusto!

Mama was always bustling around, replenishing the pots of chicken paprikas or stuffed cabbage, or seeing that plenty of coffee was ready, or preparing her marvellous pastries. A doughnut called fánk (pronounced *farnk*) was one of her specialties. We make

that in our Country Host kitchens today and still use Mama's brass pastry wheel and the rolling pin she kept especially for her delicate strudel. My sons spent many summers with their Deme grandparents. They both knew how to make noodles and chicken soup and fánk at an early age.

Chicken Paprika with Dumplings or Grated Noodles

1 ONION,
COARSELY CHOPPED

4 TABLESPOONS SWEET BUTTER

1 TABLESPOON PAPRIKA

1 TEASPOON BLACK PEPPER

2 TABLESPOONS SALT

4- TO 5-POUND CHICKEN,
CUT INTO SERVING PIECES

1½ CUPS WATER

1 PINT SOUR CREAM

DUMPLINGS (THIS PAGE) OR

GRATED NOODLES (PAGE 55)

In a large pot, brown onion in butter, then add seasonings. Brown the chicken for 10 minutes. Add water, cover and simmer slowly until tender, approximately 45 to 50 minutes. Remove chicken.

Add sour cream to cooking liquid and blend until smooth. Add dumplings. Arrange chicken on top. Heat through and serve.

6 SERVINGS

Dumplings

3 EGGS,
WELL BEATEN

3 CUPS ALL-PURPOSE FLOUR

1 TABLESPOON SALT

½ CUP WATER

Mix all the ingredients and beat with a spoon until all flour is incorporated. Drop batter by the teaspoonful into a pot of boiling salted water (about 2 quarts of water with 2 teaspoons salt). Cook about 10 minutes. The dumplings will float to the top when done. Drain and rinse with cold water. Drain again.

Grated Noodles (Tarhonya)

2 CUPS ALL-PURPOSE FLOUR,
SIFTED

2 EGGS

½ TEASPOON SALT

4 TABLESPOONS BUTTER

3 CUPS CHICKEN STOCK

SALT AND PEPPER

Mix flour, eggs, and salt together. Add only enough water to make a stiff dough. Knead dough thoroughly and form into a ball. Grate on the medium side of a grater. Spread the noodles flat on wax paper and dry overnight.

Melt butter in a large skillet. Add dried noodles and brown for 5 to 10 minutes, stirring often to prevent burning. Gradually add stock to skillet. Cover and cook until liquid is absorbed. Season with salt and pepper.

Chicken Carousel

Mama mixed up the word casserole with carousel. We still call this dish Chicken Carousel.

A 3- TO 4-POUND CHICKEN,
CUT INTO SERVING PIECES

¼ POUND SLICED BACON

4 POTATOES,
PEELED AND SLICED

2 LARGE TOMATOES,
THINLY SLICED

2 LARGE ONIONS,
THINLY SLICED

1 GREEN PEPPER,
THINLY SLICED

½ CUP SOUR CREAM

SALT AND PEPPER

BREAD CRUMBS

Sprinkle chicken pieces with salt. Line the bottom of a 4-quart casserole dish with bacon. Add a layer of potatoes, a layer of chicken, tomatoes, onions, and peppers. Sprinkle with salt and pepper. Repeat layering until dish is filled. Add sour cream and sprinkle with bread crumbs. Cover and bake for 1½ hours in a 375°F. oven.

4 SERVINGS

Chicken and Rice

Instead of a whole chicken, this dish can be made economically with chicken wings.

A 3-POUND CHICKEN,
CUT INTO SERVING PIECES

1 MEDIUM ONION,
DICED

4 TABLESPOONS LARD

1 TEASPOON PAPRIKA

1 CUP CARROTS,
DICED

1 SPRIG PARSLEY (ROOT AND GREENS),
CHOPPED

2 CUPS WATER

SALT AND PEPPER

1 CUP RICE

In a large pot, brown onions in 2 tablespoons lard. Sprinkle in paprika, add chicken and brown it. Add carrots, parsley, water, salt and pepper. Cook until chicken and vegetables are almost tender, about 35 minutes.

Melt remaining lard in skillet. Add rice and sauté for a few minutes, add to chicken and vegetables and cook over a medium flame for 15 to 20 minutes, until rice is tender. Add more water if needed to prevent burning.

4 TO 6 SERVINGS

Chicken Cognac

A very favorite recipe. Serve with rice.

3 MEDIUM CARROTS,
PEELED AND DICED

4 STALKS CELERY,
DICED

CHICKEN STOCK

3½ TEASPOONS SALT

4 OUNCES SWEET BUTTER

4 DOUBLE CHICKEN BREASTS,
BONED AND CUT INTO CUBES

SALT AND PEPPER

1 MEDIUM ONION,
CHOPPED

2 TABLESPOONS COGNAC

½ POUND MUSHROOMS,
SLICED

WHITE SAUCE
(RECIPE FOLLOWS)

GRATED RIND OF 1 LEMON

1 TEASPOON PARSLEY,
CHOPPED

Cook carrots and celery together in just enough chicken stock to cover. (Use water if chicken stock is not available.) Add ½ teaspoon salt. Cook until tender but not overdone. Drain and set aside.

In a large frying pan, sauté chicken and onions in the butter but do not brown. Cook until chicken is white and tender. Season to taste. Transfer chicken and onions with slotted spoon to a 2-quart casserole dish. Heat cognac, flambé and pour over chicken pieces. Sauté mushrooms for 5 minutes in the liquid left from cooking the chicken. Remove with slotted spoon and sprinkle over chicken pieces. Add cooked carrots and celery. Pour white sauce over chicken and vegetables. Sprinkle with grated lemon rind and parsley.

4 TO 6 SERVINGS

White Sauce for Chicken or Veal

8 TABLESPOONS SWEET BUTTER

8 TABLESPOONS FLOUR

2 CUPS CHICKEN BROTH

1 CUP SOUR CREAM

2 TABLESPOONS DRY VERMOUTH

SALT AND PEPPER

Over medium heat, melt butter in medium-sized saucepan. Add flour and cook for 5 minutes, mixing often to prevent burning. Add chicken stock gradually, stirring to prevent lumping. Cook for 5 to 10 minutes until thickened. Add sour cream and stir until smooth. Heat through but do not boil. Stir in vermouth, and season to taste.

4 TO 6 SERVINGS

Chicken Marengo

I have been asked many times to cook this dish for groups of teenagers and it has proved most successful. This is a meal in one, perfect for large groups.

1 POUND SMALL WHOLE WHITE ONIONS,
SKINNED

2 CUPS RICE

6 CUPS CHICKEN STOCK

VEGETABLE OIL

6 DOUBLE CHICKEN BREASTS,
BONED AND CUT INTO 1-INCH PIECES

½ POUND MUSHROOMS,
SLICED

2 TABLESPOONS BUTTER

1 CLOVE GARLIC,
FINELY CHOPPED

2 GREEN PEPPERS,
DICED

1 RED PEPPER,
DICED

4 TABLESPOONS ALL-PURPOSE FLOUR

A 15-OUNCE CAN WHOLE TOMATOES
WITH JUICE

1 TABLESPOON SALT

½ TEASPOON BLACK PEPPER

1 TEASPOON DRIED BASIL

¼ TEASPOON DRIED TARRAGON

1 TEASPOON DRIED OREGANO

1 CUP DRY VERMOUTH

2 TABLESPOONS PARSLEY,
CHOPPED

Put onions in a pot with enough cold water to cover. Cook until tender; set aside. (Cover the pot while the onions are cooking—they have a strong smell.)

Bring rice to full boil in 4 cups of chicken stock, then lower heat and simmer for 20 minutes. Set aside. In a large pot, heat oil and sauté chicken until tender. Do not brown. Remove from pan with slotted spoon to a dish and reserve.

Sauté mushrooms in the remaining oil. Reserve in a separate dish.

Drain off remaining oil. Melt butter in pot, then add garlic and peppers. Cook until tender. Mix in flour and cook 5 minutes. Add onions and cooking liquid. Mix well. Add chicken, salt, pepper, and spices. Mix well. Add rice and 2 remaining cups chicken stock. Simmer for 10 minutes. Add tomatoes, salt, pepper, and spices. Mix well. Add rice and 2 remaining cups chicken stock. Simmer for 10 minutes. Add vermouth and simmer 5 minutes. Remove from heat and let stand 15 or 20 minutes before serving. Check again for seasonings. Garnish with mushrooms and parsley.

8 TO 10 SERVINGS

Tarragon Chicken

This is a good cold dish that can be prepared in advance and makes an excellent dish for lunch or buffet supper.

A 6- TO 8-POUND CHICKEN

3 TO 4 SPRIGS FRESH TARRAGON

1 MEDIUM ONION

2 MEDIUM CARROTS

2 BAY LEAVES

1 TABLESPOON DRIED MIXED SPICES
(THYME, TARRAGON, AND SAVORY)

½ CUP DRY VERMOUTH

WATER

1 TABLESPOON GELATIN POWDER
PER CUP OF STOCK

Wash the chicken and pat is dry. Put two tarragon leaves inside the chicken.

In the bottom of a large pot with a cover, place the onion, carrots, and bay leaves. Add chicken, and then the mixed spices and vermouth. Cover 2/3 of the chicken with water. Cover and simmer over medium heat for about 2 hours. Allow chicken to cool, then discard the skin and remove meat from the bones. Put meat in a deep serving dish.

Strain the stock and refrigerate, removing any fat that comes to the top. Reheat the stock, measure and add the required amount of gelatin powder. Be sure the gelatin dissolves. Chop up remaining tarragon and add to aspic. Pour over the chicken pieces. Place in the refrigerator to jell.

Slice and serve.

6 TO 8 SERVINGS

Fried Chicken

Any time seems to be the right time for fried chicken. With a beautiful salad and crusty bread, it is most satisfying. I serve it with mashed potatoes and a vegetable and it is my grandson's favorite meal. This recipe is easy and the chicken is crispy delicious.

12 TO 14 PIECES OF CHICKEN
(TWO 3-POUND FRYERS)

2 CUPS FLOUR

1 TABLESPOON SALT

1 POUND LARD FOR FRYING OR
2 CUPS VEGETABLE OIL

WATERCRESS OR PARSLEY

Wipe chicken pieces dry. Mix flour and salt in a dish. Coat each piece of chicken with flour. Place in the refrigerator for 1 hour, resting the chicken in the bowl of excess flour. Flour again and set in the refrigerator for 2 hours longer. (Overnight is even better.)

In a deep fryer, heat lard or oil to 340°F. Place as many pieces of chicken in hot fat as you can without crowding. Cook 10 minutes on each side. Remove with a slotted spoon and place in a dish lined with 2 or 3 sheets of paper towels. Fry the remaining chicken. Remove from draining dish and place on serving platter. Garnish with watercress or parsley. To serve hot, remove from draining dish to a baking dish and place in a 300°F. oven until served. Do not cover—it spoils the crispiness.

6 SERVINGS

Paella

This dish is expensive because of the seafood. Nevertheless, for very special parties paella is the most colorful and beautiful dish I prepare and is a joy to eat.

2 CLOVES GARLIC,
CHOPPED

¾ CUP OLIVE OIL PLUS
2 TABLESPOONS

1 MEDIUM ONION,
CHOPPED

1 TEASPOON SWEET PAPRIKA

A 2½- TO 3-POUND FRYING CHICKEN,
CUT INTO SERVING PIECES

1 SWEET RED PEPPER,
CHOPPED

2 TABLESPOONS FRESH PARSLEY,
CHOPPED

½ TEASPOON SAFFRON

½ TEASPOON GROUND CORIANDER
OR OREGANO

½ TEASPOON TARRAGON

2 CUPS LONG-GRAINED RICE

6 CUPS CHICKEN BROTH

2 TEASPOONS SALT

6 LARGE LOBSTER TAILS,
SPLIT

2 POUNDS MUSSELS,
WASHED AND CLEANED

1 DOZEN CHERRYSTONE CLAMS,
WASHED AND CLEANED

1 POUND LARGE RAW SHRIMP,
PEELED AND DEVEINED

½ CUP DRY SHERRY

1 CUP FRESH OR FROZEN PEAS

PIMENTO STRIPS

Use a large paella pan or extra large skillet with cover. Brown garlic in oil with a pinch of salt. Remove garlic with slotted spoon. Add onion, turn flame to low and sprinkle with paprika. Add chicken, pepper, parsley, and spices. Mix thoroughly.

Add rice and stir. Pour in chicken broth and salt and bring to the boil. Reduce heat and simmer for 10 minutes.

Add lobster, mussels, clams, and shrimp and simmer uncovered for 10 minutes. Sprinkle seafood with sherry and the remaining oil. Scatter frozen peas on top, but do not mix. Cover and simmer for another 10 to 15 minutes until rice absorbs most of the liquid. Garnish with pimento strips.

10 TO 12 SERVINGS

Curried Chicken

3 TABLESPOONS ONION,
FINELY CHOPPED

1 CLOVE GARLIC,
FINELY CHOPPED

2 TABLESPOONS SWEET BUTTER

1 SMALL APPLE,
PEELED, CORED, AND CHOPPED

2 CLOVES

1 TABLESPOON CURRY POWDER

2 TABLESPOONS FLOUR

1 CUP MILK

1 CUP CHICKEN STOCK

2 MEDIUM TOMATOES,
SKINNED AND CHOPPED

1 TABLESPOON RAISINS OR
SULTANAS

2 TEASPOONS TOMATO PURÉE

2 TABLESPOONS SWEET CHUTNEY

A 1-INCH PIECE FRESH GINGER,
CHOPPED

SALT AND PEPPER

6 BONELESS CHICKEN BREASTS,
CUT INTO 1-INCH PIECES

Saute onions and garlic in butter for about 5 minutes. Add the apple and cloves and continue cooking for 2 or 3 minutes. Stir in curry powder, cook 2 minutes, then stir in flour and cook 2 minutes longer. Remove pan from heat. Stir in milk and stock, stirring continuously. Bring to a boil and cook until sauce thickens. Turn down heat. Add tomatoes, raisins, tomato purée, chutney, ginger, salt and pepper. Cover and bring back to a boil. Add chicken pieces, stir, cover and lower heat to a gentle simmer. Cook for 20 to 25 minutes until chicken is tender. Check seasonings and add more curry if desired. Serve with cooked rice.

6 SERVINGS

Chicken Salad

2 DOUBLE BREASTS OF CHICKEN

1 CUP CELERY,
COARSELY CHOPPED

2 TABLESPOONS ONION,
FINELY CHOPPED

1 GREEN PEPPER,
COARSELY CHOPPED

1 RED PEPPER,
COARSELY CHOPPED

¼ CUP SOUR CREAM

2 TEASPOONS SALT

½ TEASPOON BLACK PEPPER

2 TABLESPOONS CAPERS

1 PINT MAYONNAISE

1 TABLESPOON PARSLEY,
FINELY CHOPPED

Place chicken in a medium-sized cook pot, cover with cold water, and bring to a boil. Reduce heat and simmer, covered, until chicken is tender. Remove chicken from broth and save broth for future use. Cool. Separate meat from bones, cut into generous cubes and place in a large bowl. Add celery, onion, peppers, and sour cream. Mix. Add salt, pepper, capers, and mayonnaise. Toss well. Taste for seasonings. Garnish with parsley. Chill before serving.

NOTE: Turkey salad can be made the same way. I prefer making this salad with fresh meat rather than leftovers. Use leftover turkey for making croquettes instead. To make curried chicken or turkey salad, proceed with the above recipe but increase sour cream to ½ cup and add 1 tablespoon of medium-strength curry powder.

SERVES 4

Salted Duck in Onion Sauce

This dish reflects the simple traditional cooking of Wales. My Granny Peters served it with boiled potatoes, applesauce, and fresh green peas.

A 7- TO 8-POUND DUCK,
CLEANED

½ POUND SEA SALT

1 MEDIUM ONION,
SLICED

BLACK PEPPER,
FRESHLY GROUND

½ CUP GIBLET STOCK

½ CUP CIDER

Boil giblets in 3 cups water for 60 minutes to make stock.

Place the duck in a deep dish. Rub inside and out with some of the sea salt. Cover with a cloth and leave in refrigerator or cool place. Turn the duck and rub with salt twice a day for 2 days, then rinse well under cold water. Dry and place it in a casserole dish. Season with pepper. Combine giblet stock with cider and baste the duck. Arrange onion around the bird. Cover and cook in a 350°F. oven for 2 hours. Remove bird from casserole and place in an ovenproof dish. Baste with juices from pan and keep warm while preparing the sauce.

4 TO 6 SERVINGS

Onion Sauce

1 POUND ONIONS,
THINLY SLICED

1 CUP DUCK STOCK (MADE FROM
GIBLETS)

SALT AND PEPPER

1 TABLESPOON SWEET BUTTER

1 HEAPING TABLESPOON FLOUR

1 CUP HEAVY CREAM

Simmer onions in stock until soft. Season to taste. Strain liquid from onions and reserve.

Melt butter in saucepan, add flour, stirring for 5 minutes. Add onion liquid, stirring continuously. When mixture thickens, add onions, mix well and remove from heat. Salt and pepper to taste, add cream and stir well. Heat but do not boil. Serve over portions of salted duck.

Roast Duck and Roast Goose

Roasting a duck or goose is a little different from roasting a chicken or turkey. Over the years I have learned this simple way to assure a less fatty bird.

Prick the bird all over with a fork so the fat can escape. Place breast down in a roasting pan, adding 1 cup water to prevent sticking. Roast for 40 minutes in a 450° oven. Remove from oven and drain fat from the pan. Let the bird cool, then stuff the cavity.

I am especially fond of sage and onion stuffing or apple and prune stuffing for goose. Either is wonderful for the special times such as Christmas, when one would cook a goose.

Duck is a treat at any time. My only complaint is that several ducks have to be cooked to make enough for a hungry family. A 4- or 5-pound duck, the most tender size, is enough for only 4 people. Most of the meat is on the breast and legs. Its saving grace is the crispy skin that comes from roasting a duck properly. Filled with a fruit and nut stuffing, served with minted potatoes, applesauce, and a gravy made with giblets (page 66), duck makes very good eating.

Goose fat is highly valued by country people in England. Served cold with salt and pepper, it makes an excellent spread for toast. It is also used as a chest rub to ease tightness from a cold, as grease to keep leather supple, and as a moisturizer to keep cows' udders from chapping during cold weather. The down and feathers are prized for making luxurious eiderdown quilts and pillows.

Sage and Onion Stuffing

2 LARGE ONIONS,
PEELED

8 OUNCES FRESH BREAD CRUMBS

1 OUNCE SUET,
CHOPPED

1 TEASPOON DRIED SAGE

2 EGGS,
LIGHTLY BEATEN

SALT AND PEPPER

Put onions into a saucepan with 1 cup water, cover and bring to the boil. Lower heat to a simmer and cook for 20 minutes until partially tender. Remove onions from water, cool, then chop into small pieces. Transfer to a bowl, add the remainder of the ingredients. Mix well.

ENOUGH FOR A 10-POUND GOOSE
OR 2 4- TO 5-POUND DUCKS

Apple and Prune Stuffing

1 POUND PRUNES

3 TART APPLES,
PEELED, CORED, AND CHOPPED

1 CUP COOKED RICE

1 STALK CELERY,
CHOPPED

1 TABLESPOON PARSLEY,
CHOPPED

RIND AND JUICE OF 1 SMALL LEMON

PINCH OF MACE

SALT AND PEPPER

1 TEASPOON BROWN SUGAR

1 EGG,
LIGHTLY BEATEN

Cook prunes until tender. Cool and re-move pits. Mix prunes, apples, celery, and rice. Add the parsley, lemon rind and juice, mixing well. Add seasonings and brown sugar. Bind together with egg.

Cook the bird according to the direc-tions on page 64. Fill the cavity of the bird with the stuffing. Rub the skin with salt and pepper. Tie the legs together with string.

Place in a 350°F. oven and roast un-covered for 1¾ hours for duck and 2¾ hours for goose. Baste ½ hour before the end of cooking time.

ENOUGH FOR A 10-POUND GOOSE
OR 2 4- TO 5-POUND DUCKS

Fruit and Nut Stuffing

4 OUNCES DRIED APRICOTS,
SOAKED AND CHOPPED

4 MEDIUM TART APPLES,
PEELED, CORED, AND CHOPPED

4 OUNCES WALNUTS OR PECANS,
CHOPPED

12 SLICES WHITE BREAD,
TRIMMED AND MADE INTO 3 CUPS
OF BREAD CRUMBS

¼ POUND SWEET BUTTER,
MELTED

RIND OF 2 LEMONS

SALT AND PEPPER

Combine apricots, apples, walnuts, bread crumbs, and lemon rind in a bowl. Season to taste and bind with melted butter.

Cook the ducks or goose according to the directions on page 64.

Fill cavities of birds. Tie legs together. Rub skin with lemon juice. Sprinkle salt over birds and place in a deep roasting pan. Cook uncovered for 1¾ hours in a 350°F. oven. Baste ½ hour before the birds are finished cooking.

ENOUGH FOR A 10-POUND GOOSE
OR 2 4- TO 5-POUND DUCKS

Turkey with Chestnut Stuffing

1½ POUNDS FRESH CHESTNUTS

2 CUPS MILK

4 SLICES WHITE BREAD,
TRIMMED AND MADE INTO 1 CUP
BREAD CRUMBS

TURKEY LIVER,
CHOPPED

2 to 3 TABLESPOONS PARSLEY,
CHOPPED

SALT AND PEPPER

3 EGG YOLKS,
LIGHTLY BEATEN

A 10-POUND TURKEY

BUTTER

4 SLICES BACON

Split skins of the chestnuts and place under a broiler for 5 minutes to loosen. Peel, place in a saucepan and cover with milk. Bring to a boil, lower to simmer and cook for 45 to 50 minutes until tender. Strain off the milk and purée chestnuts in a food mill or blender. Mix the purée with turkey liver, parsley, bread crumbs, salt and pepper. Bind the stuffing with the egg yolks.

Remove giblets from the turkey. Clean the bird and rub it all over with salt. Fill cavity with chestnut stuffing. Tie legs together. Place bird in a deep roasting pan. Add 1 cup water. Rub softened butter on the breast or cover with the slices of bacon. Loosely cover the breast and sides of the turkey with a piece of aluminum foil. Place in a 350°F. oven for 3 hours. Remove foil ½ hour before finished, to brown. Baste once when bird is done. Let turkey rest in roasting pan for at least 20 minutes to make carving much easier. Remove bird to platter and keep warm until served. Use turkey drippings to make giblet gravy.

To make giblet gravy for roast turkey, duck, goose, or chicken: Simmer neck, giblets, and wing tips in 1 quart lightly salted water for 1 hour. Remove from heat and set aside. After the bird is roasted, pour off fat from roasting pan. Mix remaining sediment with 4 tablespoons flour. Place pan over low flame, stirring mixture constantly for 5 minutes. Strain giblet stock, and slowly pour into roasting pan, stirring constantly. Bring to low boil, stirring, for another 5 minutes. Season to taste.

6 SERVINGS

Old-Fashioned Chicken Stew

2 2½-POUND CHICKENS,
CUT INTO SERVING PIECES

2 TABLESPOONS SWEET BUTTER

2 MEDIUM ONIONS,
QUARTERED

6 MEDIUM CARROTS,
PEELED AND CUT INTO 1-INCH
LENGTHS

6 STALKS CELERY,
CUT INTO 1-INCH LENGTHS

2 MEDIUM TOMATOES,
QUARTERED

1 BUNCH PARSLEY

3 SMALL ZUCCHINI,
CUT INTO ¼-INCH SLICES

6 MEDIUM POTATOES,
PEELED AND QUARTERED

1 TABLESPOON SALT

¼ TEASPOONS PEPPER

In a large pot, lightly brown chicken in butter. Add all vegetables except the potatoes. Add salt and pepper. Add enough chicken stock or water to cover vegetables. Bring to the boil. Cover, lower the heat and simmer for 1 hour.

Add potatoes and more liquid if necessary. Cover and cook for 35 to 40 minutes more until potatoes are done. Remove from heat and allow to stand for 15 minutes with lid on before serving. The potatoes will thicken the liquid.

6 TO 8 SERVINGS

Veal Medallions

I buy whole legs of veal and cut them down myself. It is the only way one can afford to use large quantities of veal. I cut the eye round to make veal medallions, the bottom round for a roast, the top round for cutlets or scallopini, shin meat for stew, and leftovers are ground up for patties.

2 EYES OF VEAL,
APPROXIMATELY 1 TO 1½
POUNDS EACH

¼ POUND SWEET BUTTER

3 SHALLOTS,
FINELY CHOPPED

1 CUP SOUR CREAM

½ POUND MUSHROOMS,
SLICED

SALT AND PEPPER

CHOPPED PARSLEY

Slice veal into ¼-inch pieces and make two or three tiny cuts around the edge of each medallion to prevent edges from curling during cooking. Melt butter in a heavy skillet. Lightly sauté shallots, add medallions and cook over a medium heat 5 minutes on each side. Season to taste. Remove meat to a warm platter and keep warm.

Sauté the mushrooms in the leftover liquid for about 5 minutes. Remove with a slotted spoon and spread over the medallions. Reduce the remaining liquid and spoon over veal. Spoon tablespoons of sour cream down the center of the dish. Garnish with parsley.

6 SERVINGS

Veal Collops

2 POUNDS VEAL,
CUT INTO LARGE CHUNKS

2 EGGS,
WELL BEATEN

BREAD CRUMBS

SALT AND PEPPER

LARD OR SHORTENING
FOR FRYING

Dip veal into egg, roll in bread crumbs, and season with salt and pepper. Using a deep fryer, heat lard or vegetable shortening to 340°F. Fry collops for 10 to 12 minutes, or until golden brown. Serve with a green salad and crusty bread.

4 SERVINGS

Veal Stew

1 LARGE ONION,
CHOPPED

2 TABLESPOONS LARD

1 TABLESPOON PARSLEY,
CHOPPED

1 TEASPOON PAPRIKA

1 TEASPOON SALT

¼ TEASPOON BLACK PEPPER

2 POUNDS VEAL SHOULDER,
CUBED

½ CUP WATER

½ POUND MUSHROOMS,
SLICED

1 TABLESPOON FLOUR

1 CUP SOUR CREAM

In a medium pot, brown onion in lard. Add parsley, paprika, salt, pepper, veal, and water. Cover and cook for 1 hour.

Add mushrooms and cook until tender, about 10 minutes. Blend in flour and cook for 5 minutes. Add sour cream and stir well. Remove from heat and serve with rice.

4 TO 6 SERVINGS

Stuffed Breast of Veal

4 POUNDS BREAST OF VEAL,
WITH A POCKET FOR STUFFING

SALT AND PEPPER

1 SMALL ONION,
CHOPPED

2 TABLESPOONS BUTTER

1 CUP BREAD CRUMBS

1 TEASPOON MARJORAM OR OREGANO

1 TEASPOON THYME

1 TEASPOON SALT

¼ TEASPOON PEPPER

1 EGG,
LIGHTLY BEATEN

½ CUP WATER

Wipe veal dry and lightly sprinkle with salt and pepper. Sauté onions in butter until soft and remove from heat. Add bread crumbs, spices, and egg. Mix well.

Fill the pocket in the veal with stuffing. Place in a shallow roasting pan, add water and roast in a 350°F. oven for 1½ hours. Baste once or twice. To serve, slice down the ribs, allowing 2 ribs for each slice.

4 SERVINGS

Breaded Veal Cutlets

1 TEASPOON SALT

¼ TEASPOON PEPPER

1 CUP FLOUR

2 POUNDS VEAL CUTLETS
(ASK BUTCHER TO POUND THIN)

2 EGGS,
BEATEN

SEASONED BREAD CRUMBS

VEGETABLE OR PEANUT OIL
FOR FRYING

LEMON SLICES

Combine salt, pepper, and flour in shallow dish. Dry each cutlet, dip in flour, then into beaten egg, then into seasoned bread crumbs. In a shallow frying pan, heat approximately ½-inch of oil. Cook cutlets about 5 minutes on each side until golden brown. Remove from pan to heated platter and garnish with lemon slices.

4 SERVINGS

Veal and Ham Pie

RAISED PASTRY (PAGE 198)

1 POUND VEAL TENDERLOIN,
CUT INTO CUBES

6 OUNCES SMOKED HAM,
CUT INTO CUBES

2 HARD-BOILED EGGS,
SHELLED

½ CUP WATER

½ TEASPOON GRATED LEMON PEEL

SALT AND PEPPER

EGG WASH

1 TEASPOON UNFLAVORED GELATIN

½ TEASPOON MEAT EXTRACT

Prepare the pastry.

Mix veal and ham together. Add lemon rind, salt and pepper. Mix again. Roll out two-thirds of pastry and line a 1-pound bread pan. Place half of the meat mixture onto the pastry. Place eggs on top of meat and cover with remaining meat. Add three tablespoons of water. Turn the top edges of the pastry over the meat and brush around the edges with water. Roll out remaining pastry and cover top of pie. Turn in and press down all around the edges.

Crimp as for a pie and be sure the top is sealed. Cut a hole in the center of the pie crust. Brush crust with egg wash, which is made by beating an egg well and mixing thoroughly with 2 teaspoons cold water. Decorate top with pastry cutouts and brush again with egg wash. Place pie on a baking sheet, in case of drippings while cooking, and bake in a 375°F. oven for 2 to 2½ hours or until golden. Remove pie from oven and let cool.

Melt gelatin in remaining water and stir in meat extract. Cool gelatin and pour mixture through hole in top of pie or force in with a basting bulb. Refrigerate before serving.

6 SERVINGS

Stuffed Cabbage

1 LARGE HEAD CABBAGE

1 LARGE ONION,
CHOPPED

3 TABLESPOONS SWEET BUTTER

½ POUND GROUND VEAL

½ POUND GROUND PORK

½ POUND GROUND BEEF

2 TABLESPOONS SALT

1 TABLESPOON PAPRIKA

1 TEASPOON BLACK PEPPER

1½ CUPS UNCOOKED LONG-GRAINED
RICE

1 POUND SAUERKRAUT,
WASHED AND DRAINED (OPTIONAL)

6 MEDIUM TOMATOES,
PEELED AND CUT INTO PIECES OR
1 LARGE (NO. 2) CAN WHOLE
TOMATOES

1 CUP TOMATO SAUCE

1 CUP SOUR CREAM

Core cabbage and cover with boiling water. Cook for 5 minutes. As the leaves wilt, cut them from the cabbage until all leaves have been removed. Drain and pare the thick center vein on each leaf. Save the parings.

Using a large heavy skillet, brown the onion in the butter. Remove from heat. Add meats, seasonings, and raw rice. Mix thoroughly.

Place 1 tablespoon of meat mixture on each cabbage leaf. Roll up and tuck in each end to form a roll. Place cabbage rolls in a heavy pot in layers. Cover two-thirds full with water.

Arrange sauerkraut on top. Add tomatoes, sauce, and cabbage parings. Cover and cook slowly for 1½ hours until rice is tender. Stir once or twice to prevent sticking. Add sour cream and cook 5 minutes. Let stand for 10 minutes before serving.

NOTE: Pork or veal bones placed on the bottom of the pot before the cabbage rolls go in prevent the rolls from burning, but I simply shake the pot from side to side when necessary. Smoked sausage is an excellent addition, too. Place chunks on top of the sauerkraut and continue with the recipe. Stuffed cabbage can also be placed in a covered pot and baked in a 350°F. oven for 2 hours.

6 TO 8 SERVINGS

Beef Goulash with Egg Dumplings

Delicious on a cold winter day.

2 POUNDS BOTTOM ROUND OF BEEF,
CUT INTO 1-INCH SQUARES

2 TABLESPOONS SALT

2 MEDIUM ONIONS,
FINELY CHOPPED

4 TABLESPOONS LARD

1 TABLESPOON PAPRIKA

6 MEDIUM CARROTS,
SCRAPED AND SLICED INTO
¼-INCH ROUNDS

4 PARSLEY SPRIGS (ROOTS),
CHOPPED

2 QUARTS WATER

8 MEDIUM POTATOES,
PEELED AND DICED

½ TEASPOON BLACK PEPPER

6 TABLESPOONS FLOUR

SALT

1 EGG

Sprinkle beef with 1 tablespoon salt and mix. In a large heavy pot, brown onion in the lard. Add beef and paprika. Cover and let the beef simmer over a medium low flame in its juices for 1 hour. Stir once or twice. Add carrots and parsley roots. Cover and simmer for 30 minutes. Add water, potatoes, and remaining salt. Cook until potatoes are done. Add pepper.

Prepare egg dumplings: Add flour and a pinch of salt to the unbeaten egg. Mix well. Let batter stand for 30 minutes. Drop by teaspoonfuls into goulash. Simmer for 5 minutes after dumplings rise to surface.

8 TO 10 SERVINGS

Roast Beef

A choice eye round of beef weighs 4 to 5 pounds. It is wise to use it for roast beef because there is very little waste. Serve the meat hot and save leftovers for cold platters or sandwiches. Ground roast beef makes a delicious meat or shepherd's pie.

4 TO 5 POUND EYE ROUND OF BEEF

SALT

BLACK PEPPER,
FRESHLY GROUND

½ CUP WATER

Preheat oven to 375°F.

Place meat in a roasting pan. Sprinkle generously with salt and pepper. Add water to pan. Roast uncovered for 55 minutes for rare, 1¼ hours for medium, 1½ hours for well done. Remove and let stand for 10 minutes before slicing. Save pan drippings for gravy (recipe follows).

5 TO 6 SERVINGS

Gravy

½ CUP ALL-PURPOSE FLOUR

4 CUPS BROWN STOCK

SALT

Mix flour with the drippings in roasting pan. Place roasting pan over a medium flame. Slowly add brown stock or potato water to flour mixture. Stir well, cooking for 10 to 15 minutes until smooth. Salt to taste.

NOTE: If you don't have brown stock or potato water, use water with a teaspoon of Bovril or Marmite.

Steak and Kidney Pie

2 POUNDS SIRLOIN STEAK,
CUT INTO CUBES

¾ POUND BEEF KIDNEY,
CUT INTO CUBES

2 TABLESPOONS LEMON JUICE

1 CUP WATER

1 TEASPOON SALT

2 MEDIUM ONIONS,
COARSELY CHOPPED

2 TABLESPOONS BUTTER

4 MEDIUM-SIZED CARROTS,
PEELED AND CUT INTO
½-INCH CIRCLES

½ POUND MUSHROOMS,
SLICED

4 CUPS BROWN STOCK OR WATER

4 TABLESPOONS WORCESTERSHIRE
SAUCE

4 TABLESPOONS FLOUR

2 TEASPOONS SALT

¼ TEASPOON BLACK PEPPER

1 TEASPOON BOUQUET GARNI (THYME,
BASIL, AND BAY LEAF)

DOUBLE REGULAR SHORTCRUST
PASTRY RECIPE (PAGE 195)

1 EGG,
BEATEN

Marinate kidneys in lemon juice water, and salt for 45 minutes. Sauté onions in butter in a large heavy pan. Add steak and drained kidneys. Cook for 10 minutes. Add carrots, mushrooms, stock, and Worcestershire sauce. Mix together, bring to a boil and then lower heat to a simmer. Cover the pot and cook for 1½ hours.

Mix flour with some liquid from pot—just enough to make smooth consistency. Add this to the meat mixture and stir well to prevent lumps. Add salt, pepper and bouquet garni. Mix again. Remove from heat.

Prepare pastry and roll out. Place meat mixture in a large dish. Cover with pastry. Crimp edges of pastry to seal. Brush pastry with egg, make 2 slits in top and decorate with pastry design. Brush with egg again. Bake in center of a 375°F. oven for 1 hour and 10 minutes, or until pastry is golden brown.

8 SERVINGS

Steak, Kidney, and Oyster Pie

½ POUND BEEF KIDNEY,
CUT INTO 1-INCH PIECES

2 TABLESPOONS LEMON JUICE

1 CUP WATER

1 TEASPOON SALT

2 TABLESPOONS FLOUR
SEASONED WITH ¼ TEASPOON
EACH OF SALT AND PEPPER

1½ POUNDS SIRLOIN STEAK,
CUT INTO 1-INCH PIECES

1 TABLESPOON PARSLEY,
CHOPPED

1 TABLESPOON LARD

1 MEDIUM ONION,
CHOPPED

1½ CUPS STOCK

1 DOZEN OYSTERS (AND LIQUID),
CHOPPED

SALT AND PEPPER

DOUBLE RECIPE PUFF PASTRY
OR FLAKY PASTRY
(PAGES 196 AND 198)

1 EGG,
BEATEN

Soak kidneys for 45 minutes in lemon juice, water, and salt. Discard liquid. Dust steak and kidney pieces with seasoned flour. Sprinkle parsley over meat. Melt lard in a heavy pot and sauté onions and meat until brown. Add stock and bring to a boil over medium heat. Lower heat to a simmer and continue cooking for 1½ hours.

Put mixture into a 2-quart pie dish. Add oysters and liquid. Stir once or twice. Season to taste. Roll out pastry to cover pie. Make a design of cut out pastry leaves for top of pastry. Crimp pastry around edges to seal. Brush with beaten egg. Bake in a 400°F. oven for 1 hour, or until golden.

6 TO 8 SERVINGS

Stuffed Peppers

1 MEDIUM ONION,
CHOPPED

4 TABLESPOONS BUTTER

1½ POUNDS ROUND BEEF STEAK,
CHOPPED

1 CUP COOKED LONG-GRAIN RICE

2 CUPS TOMATO SAUCE OR
TWO 8-OUNCE CANS

6 LARGE GREEN PEPPERS,
SEEDED AND CORED

2 MEDIUM TOMATOES,
SKINNED AND CHOPPED

SALT AND PEPPER

2 TABLESPOONS FLOUR

½ CUP WATER

2 TABLESPOONS SOUR CREAM

Sauté onion in butter until golden brown. Remove from heat.

In a bowl, mix meat, onion, rice, 2 tablespoons of tomato sauce, and seasonings.

Fill each pepper with meat mixture. Spread tomatoes over peppers and add remaining tomato sauce. Cover and bake in a 350°F. oven for 1 hour. Remove cover and continue baking for 35 to 40 minutes longer. Serve peppers with the cooking liquid. For a sauce, remove peppers with slotted spoon. Thicken liquid with flour mixed with ½ cup water. Cook over a low flame until thickened, stirring constantly to prevent lumping. Mix in sour cream and stir until smooth. Spoon sauce over peppers and serve.

6 SERVINGS

Shepherd's Pie

A good dish for leftover beef.

4 TABLESPOONS BUTTER

½ LARGE ONION,
CHOPPED

1½ POUNDS LEFTOVER ROAST BEEF,
GROUND

4 CUPS BEEF STOCK
(PAGE 201)

4 LARGE CARROTS,
GRATED

½ CUP FLOUR

1 TABLESPOON WORCESTERSHIRE
SAUCE

2 CUPS MASHED POTATOES

Melt butter in a saucepan. Sauté onion and beef for 3 to 4 minutes. Add beef stock and simmer for 15 minutes. Add carrots and simmer for 10 minutes. Thicken with flour and water mixed to a smooth paste. Stir and cook for 10 more minutes. Mix in Worcestershire sauce. Remove from heat and let cool.

Cover meat with potatoes and make a pretty design with fork tines. Place casserole under the broiler for 10 minutes, or until potato topping is brown. For color, sprinkle with chopped parsley before serving.

6 TO 8 SERVINGS

Beef Burgundy

Beef Burgundy tastes better the next day. Place the covered dish in a 350°F. oven for 45 minutes to reheat. Serve with buttered broad noodles.

2 POUNDS RUMP STEAK
OR BOTTOM ROUND,
CUT INTO 2-INCH CUBES

½ CUP FLOUR

1 TEASPOON SALT

¼ TEASPOON PEPPER

4 TABLESPOONS SWEET BUTTER

2 LARGE ONIONS,
COARSELY CHOPPED

¼ CUP COGNAC

8 MEDIUM CARROTS,
PEELED AND DICED

8 STALKS CELERY,
DICED

2 CUPS DRY BURGUNDY

½ TEASPOON OREGANO

¼ TEASPOON BASIL

2 BAY LEAVES,
CRUSHED

SALT AND PEPPER

Lightly coat meat in flour seasoned with salt and pepper. Melt butter in heavy frying pan and sauté onions. Remove onions with slotted spoon and place in large casserole. Brown the meat in onion butter, then transfer to casserole. Warm Cognac, light it and pour over meat. Add carrots, celery, Burgundy, and seasonings. Cover casserole and place in 350°F. oven for 3 hours or until meat is fork tender.

Check once about 2 hours into the cooking time. If you want more liquid, add ½ cup water.

6 SERVINGS

Beef Stroganoff

2 POUNDS SIRLOIN BEEF,
CUT INTO 2-x½-INCH STRIPS

1 CUP FLOUR SEASONED WITH
1 TABLESPOON SALT

2 MEDIUM ONIONS,
CHOPPED

4 TABLESPOONS SWEET BUTTER

½ POUND MUSHROOMS,
SLICED

1 PINT SOUR CREAM

4 TABLESPOONS TOMATO PASTE

6 TABLESPOONS WORCESTERSHIRE
SAUCE

Coat meat with flour. In a deep pot, sauté onions in 2 tablespoons butter and add meat. Brown lightly, then add enough water to cover meat pieces. Bring to a boil then lower heat and simmer for 45 minutes to 1 hour, or until meat is fork tender.

Sauté mushrooms lightly in 2 tablespoons butter. Add to meat. Combine sour cream, tomato paste, and Worcestershire sauce and add to meat and mushrooms. Stir well. Heat thoroughly, but do not boil. Serve over rice or noodles.

6 SERVINGS

Pork and Sauerkraut

1 ONION,
CHOPPED

2 TABLESPOONS LARD

2 POUNDS FRESH PORK TENDERLOIN,
CUT INTO 1-INCH CUBES

1 TEASPOON SWEET PAPRIKA

SALT AND PEPPER

2 CUPS WATER

1½ POUNDS SAUERKRAUT,
THOROUGHLY WASHED

1 CUP SOUR CREAM

In a medium pot, brown onion in lard. Add pork and paprika, salt and pepper. Add water. Cover and cook over a low heat for about 30 minutes. Add sauerkraut and cook 25 minutes or until meat is tender. Add sour cream, mix well, and heat thoroughly.

4 SERVINGS

Casserole of Pork and Apples

1 POUND LEAN PORK, CUBED

1 TABLESPOON LARD

1 ONION, CHOPPED

1 TEASPOON PAPRIKA

1 TEASPOON SALT

2 CUPS LONG-GRAINED COOKED RICE

4 MEDIUM TART APPLES, PEELED, CORED AND THINLY SLICED

1 CUP SOUR CREAM

Melt lard, add onion and lightly brown. Add paprika, pork, and salt. Mix together. Cook over a low flame for 1 hour, adding a little water from time to time. In a casserole dish arrange layers of meat, cooked rice and apples. Continue until all ingredients are used. Pour sour cream over the top and bake in a 350° oven for 1 hour, or until top is browned.

4 SERVINGS

Kidneys with Rice

5 OR 6 PORK OR LAMB KIDNEYS

1 TABLESPOON VINEGAR

4 TABLESPOONS LARD

1 ONION, CHOPPED

½ TEASPOON BLACK PEPPER

1 TEASPOON PAPRIKA

SALT

3 CUPS COOKED RICE

Wash kidneys and discard any skin or membrane. Soak for 1 hour in enough water to cover, acidulated with vinegar. Drain. Place kidneys in a small saucepan and cover with cold water, bring to a boil, then lower heat and simmer for 30 minutes. Remove from heat, drain, cool and slice.

In large skillet, melt lard and sauté onions. Add seasonings and the kidneys. Cook for 10 minutes and add the cooked rice. Mix well and heat thoroughly before serving.

4 SERVINGS

Lobscouse

This stew that is popular in Lancashire and Yorkshire is the first meat dish I made as a child.

1 POUND MUTTON, LAMB SHANKS
OR SHOULDER,
CUT INTO 1-INCH CUBES

1 POUND STEWING BEEF

2 CUPS BEEF STOCK OR 2 CUPS WATER
WITH 1 TEASPOON BEEF EXTRACT

1 TABLESPOON SALT

¼ TEASPOON BLACK PEPPER

1 TEASPOON THYME

3 LARGE CARROTS,
CUT INTO 1-INCH PIECES

1 MEDIUM TURNIP,
CUT INTO 1-INCH PIECES

3 LARGE ONIONS,
COARSELY CHOPPED

6 LARGE POTATOES,
PEELED AND HALVED

Place meat in a large pot with stock and seasonings. Bring to a boil, lower heat, cover and simmer for 1 hour, or until meat is tender. Add vegetables and simmer for 1 hour. Add a little water if necessary but the liquid should be thick.

6 SERVINGS

Preparation of Sweetbreads

The best sweetbreads to buy are veal. Lamb is acceptable as a second choice and less expensive. Soak sweetbreads in cold water as soon as possible after purchasing, for at least 1 hour. Parboil sweetbreads in 1 quart of water, seasoned with 1 tablespoon of vinegar and one teaspoon of salt. Boil over medium heat for 20 minutes. Drain and plunge into cold water to firm up. Remove any membranes, veins, and strings. Now the sweetbreads are ready to use.

Creamed Sweetbreads

2 PAIRS PREPARED SWEETBREADS

4 TABLESPOONS BUTTER

4 TABLESPOONS FLOUR

2 CUPS CREAM OR HALF-AND-HALF

SALT AND PEPPER

1 TEASPOON PARSLEY
CHOPPED

Cut sweetbreads into small pieces.

Make the sauce: Melt butter and stir in flour. Cook mixture over low heat for 8 to 10 minutes. Add cream, stirring constantly to prevent lumping. Continue cooking over low heat until sauce thickens. Add sweetbreads. Season with salt and pepper. Serve over toast garnished with parsley.

2 TO 3 SERVINGS

Fried Sweetbreads

2 PAIRS PREPARED SWEETBREADS,
CUT INTO ¼-INCH SLICES

SALT AND PEPPER

1 EGG,
BEATEN

BREAD CRUMBS

VEGETABLE OIL FOR FRYING

2 TABLESPOONS FLOUR

2 TABLESPOONS BUTTER

1 CUP MILK

LEMON SLICES

Season sweetbreads with salt and pepper. Dip into egg and then into bread crumbs. Fry in oil heated to 340°F. until golden brown. Remove with slotted spoon. Keep hot.

Make a white sauce: melt butter and add flour. Cook over medium heat for 5 minutes. Gradually add the milk to mixture, stirring constantly to prevent lumping. Continue cooking until sauce thickens. Add salt and pepper to taste. Serve sweetbreads garnished with lemon slices, and with the sauce served separately.

2 SERVINGS

Tripe and Onion Stew

2 POUNDS HONEYCOMB
TRIPE

2 LARGE ONIONS,
SLICED

1½ CUPS MILK

2 TABLESPOONS BUTTER

2 TABLESPOONS FLOUR

SALT AND PEPPER

1/8 TEASPOON NUTMEG

Soak tripe in cold water for 1 hour.

Cut the tripe into thin strips about 3 inches long. Simmer tripe and onions in milk until tender. Melt butter in a pan and add flour, cooking without browning. Strain milk from the tripe and onions. Gradually add liquid to the butter and flour, stirring and simmering until thickened. Season with 1 teaspoon salt, a shake of pepper, and nutmeg. Add tripe and onions, then heat thoroughly. Serve with mashed potatoes.

6 SERVINGS

Notes

Vegetables and Salads

Meatless days are not so bad when they feature wonderful vegetable pie and some cooked fresh vegetables alongside it. Potatoes are considered a main dish in the British Isles. Every day potatoes are eaten in one form or another —sausage and mash, fish and chips, scalloped, baked, creamed, boiled, or fried. The best potatoes I've ever eaten were the ones in my childhood that we would throw into the glowing embers of a Guy Fawkes bonfire. Guy Fawkes Night is celebrated in England on November 5 and it is similar to the Fourth of July. Guy Fawkes attempted to blow up the London Houses of Parliament with gunpowder in 1605. The date is celebrated because his attempt was thwarted. We would spend several days before the holiday collecting wood and garden debris for the huge bonfire on that night. Finally, on November 5, fireworks would be set off, and we would stand around the blaze, our breath visible in the cold, drinking mugs of hot cocoa. When the embers of the fire glowed hot we each threw in a potato. As soon as they became black and crispy we would poke them out of the fire with a long stick. Everyone wore woolen gloves and the hot potato warmed our hands and satisfied our tummies. When the fireworks ended and the fire had died down, we would head for home, dirty and streaky, but happy.

Vegetable Pie

2 CARROTS,
DICED

2 STALKS CELERY,
DICED

1 ZUCCHINI,
SLICED INTO ¼-INCH ROUNDS

1 GREEN PEPPER,
DICED

1 RED PEPPER,
DICED

COLD WATER

1 TEASPOON SALT

1 CUP CHEESE SAUCE
(RECIPE FOLLOWS)

1 POUND CREAMED POTATOES

BUTTER

CHEDDAR CHEESE

PARSLEY,
CHOPPED

Cook the vegetables until tender in water to cover and salt. Drain and mix with cheese sauce. Ladle the mixture into a medium-sized casserole dish. Cover with creamed potatoes (made by creaming boiled potatoes with butter and milk). Make a design on top with either fork tines or some of the creamed potatoes forced through a pastry bag. Dot the top with small pieces of butter and a sprinkling of grated cheddar cheese. Bake in a 400°F. oven for 20 to 25 minutes, or until potatoes are browned. Remove from oven and garnish with parsley.

4 TO 6 SERVINGS

Cheese Sauce

1 TABLESPOON BUTTER

1 TABLESPOON FLOUR

SALT AND PEPPER

1 CUP MILK

4 OUNCES CHEDDAR CHEESE,
GRATED

½ TEASPOON MUSTARD

Melt butter, remove from heat, and stir in flour. Cook gently for a few minutes, but do not brown. Remove pan from heat and gradually blend in milk. Bring mixture to a boil and cook, stirring with a wooden spoon until smooth. Stir in cheese and mustard. Season to taste.

Potato and Cabbage Casserole

2 POUNDS POTATOES,
PEELED AND SLICED

1 POUND CABBAGE,
FINELY CHOPPED

2 LARGE TOMATOES,
PEELED AND CHOPPED

2 TABLESPOONS UNSALTED BUTTER

¼ POUND CHEDDAR CHEESE,
DICED

SALT AND PEPPER

Boil potatoes in just enough water to cover until tender. Drain, being careful not to break the potato pieces.

In a skillet, sauté cabbage in butter. Add chopped tomatoes and cook for 5 minutes. Combine cabbage mixture with the potatoes. Season to taste. Serve immediately.

4 TO 6 SERVINGS

Paprikas Potatoes

This is a simple recipe that I learned from Mama many years ago.

3 TABLESPOONS LARD

2 TABLESPOONS PAPRIKA

5 POTATOES,
PEELED AND SLICED

¾ CUP WATER

SALT AND PEPPER

Melt lard in a heavy skillet. Add potatoes, paprika, salt and pepper to taste. Cover and cook over a medium flame for 15 minutes. Gradually add water and continue cooking until potatoes are soft but not mushy. Total cooking time should be about 25 minutes.

4 SERVINGS

Potato Pancakes I

These pancakes are a wonderful accompaniment for pot roast or with bacon and eggs.

1 CUP ALL-PURPOSE FLOUR

1 TEASPOON BAKING POWDER

2 CUPS MASHED POTATOES

PINCH NUTMEG

2 TABLESPOONS BROWN SUGAR

1 TABLESPOON BUTTER,
MELTED

½ CUP MILK

Sift flour and baking powder into a large bowl. Add mashed potatoes and mix thoroughly. Add nutmeg, sugar, and butter. Gradually mix in milk. Stir all ingredients together thoroughly to form a stiff dough. Roll dough out on a lightly floured board to about 1-inch thickness. Cut into rounds or triangles and cook on a lightly greased medium-hot griddle. Cook on one side 6 to 7 minutes and turn and brown the other side. Serve hot with butter.

4 SERVINGS

Potato Pancakes II

I serve these with pot roast or just with applesauce for a light luncheon dish.

3 CUPS RAW POTATOES,
GRATED

1 TABLESPOON SALT

DASH OF BLACK PEPPER

1 EGG,
LIGHTLY BEATEN

1½ CUPS FLOUR

¼ CUP LARD

Mix together potatoes, salt, pepper, egg, and flour. Heat lard in a heavy skillet. Test for correct heat by dropping a teaspoon of the batter into the fat. If fat sizzles around the edges of the batter, it is ready. Drop tablespoons of batter into the hot fat and fry both sides until golden brown.

4 SERVINGS

Scalloped Potatoes

There are several ways to making scalloped potatoes—this happens to be my favorite. Served with a green salad, it is hearty enough for a main meal.

6 MEDIUM POTATOES,
BOILED IN SKINS

8 HARD-BOILED EGGS,
SHELLED AND CUT INTO
¼-INCH SLICES

8 TABLESPOONS BUTTER,
MELTED

DRY BREAD CRUMBS

1 CUP SOUR CREAM

SALT AND PEPPER

Grease a casserole dish with 2 tablespoons of butter. Sprinkle with bread crumbs. Skin boiled potatoes and cut into ¼-inch slices. In the casserole, put layers of potatoes, eggs, seasonings, remaining butter, and bread crumbs. Continue until all ingredients are used. Cover with sour cream. Bake in 350°F. oven for 1 hour, or until golden.

4 SERVINGS

Carrots and Peas with Fresh Mint

2 CUPS CARROTS,
CUT INTO ¼-INCH SLICES

1 CUP FRESH OR FROZEN PEAS

1 SMALL BUNCH FRESH MINT

SALT AND PEPPER

2 TABLESPOONS BUTTER

SUGAR

Put carrots into a medium-sized pot, cover with cold water, bring to a boil, and cook for 10 minutes. Add peas and 2 sprigs of mint. Boil for 5 minutes. Drain, add salt and pepper to taste. Dot with butter. Transfer to a shallow casserole dish and sprinkle with sugar. Place in a 350° F. oven until sugar melts, about 5 minutes.

Garnish with fresh mint leaves.

4 TO 6 SERVINGS

Carrots and Zucchini

6 CARROTS,
SCRAPED AND CUT INTO
JULIENNE STRIPS

3 MEDIUM ZUCCHINI,
CUT INTO ¼-INCH CIRCLES

1 QUART WATER

SALT AND PEPPER

2 TABLESPOONS BUTTER

DASH OF GRATED NUTMEG

1 TEASPOON LEMON PEEL,
GRATED

1 TEASPOON PARSLEY,
CHOPPED

Place carrots in a medium-sized saucepan and cover with cold water. Bring to a boil and cook for 10 minutes. Drain and set aside.

Bring 1 quart water to a boil, add zucchini and boil for 5 minutes. Drain. Arrange carrots in a serving dish, cover with zucchini and gently mix the vegetables together. Sprinkle with salt and pepper, dot with butter and grated nutmeg. Garnish with lemon peel and parsley.

4 SERVINGS

Baked Squash

2 MEDIUM ONIONS,
CHOPPED

2 TABLESPOONS BUTTER

¾ POUND LEFTOVER COOKED
GROUND MEAT

½ CUP FRESH BREAD CRUMBS

GOOD PINCH SAGE

SALT AND PEPPER

1 MEDIUM-SIZED ACORN OR
BUTTERNUT SQUASH

2 TABLESPOONS BEEF DRIPPINGS
OR LARD

Sauté onions until golden in 2 table-spoons butter.

Mix meat, onions, bread crumbs, sage, salt, and pepper. Cut off one end of the squash, like a cap. Scrape out any seeds. Fill squash with the meat mixture. Replace the cap and secure with a skewer. Melt the drippings or lard in a roasting pan. Put the squash into the pan and roast for 1 hour in a 400°F. oven. Cut into generous slices to serve.

2 TO 3 SERVINGS

Scalloped Cabbage

1 SMALL HEAD OF CABBAGE,
SHREDDED

1 TEASPOON SALT

2 CUPS GRATED CHEDDAR CHEESE

1½ CUPS WHITE SAUCE (PAGE 92)

¾ CUP FRESH BREAD CRUMBS

2 TABLESPOONS BUTTER

Cover cabbage with cold water and salt and cook for 20 minutes.

Into a greased baking dish, put layers of cabbage, cheese, and white sauce until all ingredients have been used. Cover the mixture with bread crumbs, dot with butter, and bake in a 350°F. oven for 30 minutes, or until top is brown.

4 SERVINGS

Scalloped Cauliflower

1 MEDIUM CAULIFLOWER,
CUT INTO SMALL FLOWERETS

1 TEASPOON SALT

2 COOKED EGGS,
SLICED, OR 6 TABLESPOONS
CHEDDAR CHEESE,
GRATED

SALT AND PEPPER

1½ CUPS MEDIUM-THICK
WHITE SAUCE
(RECIPE FOLLOWS)

BREAD CRUMBS

CAYENNE PEPPER

Cook cauliflower in boiling water until tender, adding salt just before cooking is completed. Drain.

Grease a baking dish and place a layer of cauliflower in it, then the eggs or cheese, and finally the white sauce. Salt and pepper to taste. Cover with bread crumbs and a sprinkle of cayenne pepper. Bake in a 400°F. oven until top is browned, approximately 20 minutes.

4 SERVINGS

White Sauce for Vegetables or Fish

4 TABLESPOONS FLOUR

4 TABLESPOONS BUTTER

1½ CUPS MILK

½ TEASPOON SALT

¼ TEASPOON BLACK PEPPER

In a saucepan, melt butter, add flour and cook, stirring constantly for 5 minutes. Slowly add the milk, stirring vigorously. Simmer for 15 minutes. Add seasonings just before sauce is to be used.

YIELDS 1½ CUPS

Stuffed Onions

My Grannie always believed that onions cooked this way would help a cold.

4 LARGE SPANISH ONIONS,
PEELED

3 SLICES OF BACON,
FINELY CHOPPED

2 TABLESPOONS INSTANT OATMEAL

1 TEASPOON WORCESTERSHIRE SAUCE

1 TABLESPOON STILTON OR
DANISH BLUE CHEESE,
GRATED

¼ TEASPOON MIXED HERBS
(THYME, BASIL AND TARRAGON)

2 TABLESPOONS CHEDDAR CHEESE,
GRATED

4 TABLESPOONS WATER

½ TEASPOON MEAT EXTRACT

SALT AND PEPPER

Make two cross cuts approximately ¾-inch deep on the top of each onion. Cook in boiling salted water for 20 to 25 minutes, drain, and cool. Cut a ½-inch slice from the top of each onion. Remove centers of onions, and chop both centers and tops.

Fry bacon until crisp. Remove from heat and stir in chopped onion pulp and oatmeal. Add Worcestershire sauce, cheeses, herbs, salt and pepper to taste. Mix well.

Stuff onions with the mixture. Place in a greased casserole dish, add water and meat extract. Cover and bake in a 350°F. oven for 1½ hours.

4 SERVINGS

String Beans with Garlic

Two friends who own and operate The Sumptuary restaurant in New York City gave me this recipe. I first ate these string beans at a private party they gave served with cold venison. and sour cream. I became addicted to them and the recipe is so simple. Try it!

1 POUND FRESH STRING BEANS,
TRIMMED

¼ POUND BUTTER

2 CLOVES GARLIC,
PEELED AND PRESSED

Sauté beans in butter over medium heat until tender and brown in some spots. Do not overcook.

Transfer beans to a heated dish. Press garlic directly over beans. Toss beans lightly to distribute the garlic. Keep in a warming oven until ready to serve.

4 SERVINGS

Zucchini Salad

6 MEDIUM ZUCCHINI,
CUT INTO ¼-INCH SLICES

1 MEDIUM EGGPLANT,
PEELED AND DICED

2 GREEN PEPPERS,
SEEDED AND DICED

1 RED PEPPER,
SEEDED AND DICED

6 RIPE TOMATOES,
SKINNED AND CHOPPED

1 LARGE ONION,
CHOPPED

1 TABLESPOON BOUQUET GARNI
(THYME, TARRAGON, BASIL,
AND BAY LEAVES)

1 CUP ITALIAN DRESSING (PAGE 201)

8 OUNCES TOMATO JUICE

SALT AND PEPPER

Combine all ingredients in a large pot. Bring to a boil and lower heat. Simmer uncovered for 20 to 25 minutes or until zucchini is tender. Stir together once or twice while simmering.

Served hot or cold, this is a delicious salad.

6 SERVINGS

Cucumbers in Sour Cream

8 MEDIUM CUCUMBERS,
PEELED AND THINLY SLICED

1 TABLESPOON SALT

½ CUP WHITE VINEGAR

8 OUNCES SOUR CREAM

BLACK PEPPER,
FRESHLY GROUND

SPRINKLE OF SWEET PAPRIKA

Place cucumbers in a shallow dish and sprinkle with salt. Let stand for 1 hour, weighing them down with a large plate.

Squeeze the cucumbers, removing as much liquid as possible. Put into a bowl and sprinkle with vinegar. Add sour cream and pepper. Mix thoroughly with a wooden spoon. Taste for salt. Sprinkle with paprika. Serve cold.

8 SERVINGS

Vinegar, Cucumber, and Fresh Dill Salad

8 MEDIUM CUCUMBERS,
PEELED AND THINLY SLICED

1 TABLESPOON SALT

8 OUNCES DILL VINEGAR

1 TEASPOON SUGAR

2 TABLESPOONS SCALLION GREENS,
CHOPPED

1 TEASPOON DILL SEEDS

SALT AND PEPPER

4 SPRIGS FRESH DILL,
SNIPPED

Place cucumbers in a shallow dish, sprinkle with salt, and weigh down. Let stand for 1 hour. Squeeze the cucumbers, removing as much liquid as possible.

Toss cucumbers in a bowl with vinegar. Add sugar and mix again. Add scallions, dill seeds, salt and pepper, and fresh dill. Mix again. Chill for 1 hour before serving.

6 SERVINGS

Cole Slaw

I prefer creamy cole slaw. If a drier consistency is desired, use ½ cup sour cream and 1 cup mayonnaise.

2½ TO 3 POUNDS CABBAGE,
GRATED

5 MEDIUM CARROTS,
PEELED AND GRATED

1 SMALL ONION,
PEELED AND GRATED

3 TABLESPOONS SUGAR

1 TABLESPOON SALT

½ TEASPOON BLACK PEPPER

1 CUP WHITE OR BROWN VINEGAR

1 CUP SOUR CREAM

1 CUP MAYONNAISE

Into a large dish, combine cabbage, carrots, and onion. Sprinkle with sugar, salt, and pepper. Toss to mix. Add vinegar and mix again. Let stand for 15 minutes. Add sour cream and mayonnaise, mixing well. Chill before serving.

10 SERVINGS

Potato Salad

The best potato salad is made while potatoes are hot, allowing the seasonings to really permeate them.

3 POUNDS MEDIUM POTATOES

5 STALKS CELERY,
DICED

2 MEDIUM ONIONS,
FINELY CHOPPED

½ CUP VINEGAR

2 TABLESPOONS PARSLEY,
CHOPPED

2 CUPS MAYONNAISE

SALT AND PEPPER

Cover potatoes with cold water, bring to a boil, and cook until tender—do not overcook. Drain.

While potatoes are still hot, peel and cut into medium slices into a large bowl. Add celery and onions. Sprinkle with vinegar and toss. Add parsley and mayonnaise. Mix well, but do not mash the potatoes. Salt and pepper to taste. Chill before serving.

8 TO 10 SERVINGS

Spinach, Beet, and Orange Salad

1 POUND SPINACH

3 LARGE ORANGES,
CUT IN HALF

4 BEETS,
COOKED AND CHOPPED

4 TABLESPOONS SLIVERED ALMONDS

½ CUP ITALIAN OR FRENCH
DRESSING (PAGE 201)

Tear spinach into bite-sized pieces and place in a deep bowl. Scoop out the orange pulp and save shells. Remove white parts and seeds. Break orange segments into bite-sized pieces and combine with spinach. Add beets, almonds, and dressing. Toss to distribute dressing. Stuff salad into orange shell. Chill and sprinkle with a few almonds.

4 TO 6 SERVINGS

Notes

Baking

Afternoon tea became fashionable in England during the nineteenth century because of the long time between lunch and dinner. It is still enjoyed in the British Isles and elsewhere.

Tea is usually served at 4 P.M. along with thin slices of buttered bread, cucumber or watercress sandwiches, Madeira or seed cake, and, a great favorite of mine, Dundee fruit cake. In cold weather, toasted crumpets are served hot with lots of butter and raspberry jam.

High tea is really a suppertime meal. The working population especially in the farming areas of England are early-to-bed and early-to-rise. They enjoy hearty breakfasts, a hot dinner at midday and high tea or supper at 5 or 6 P.M. High tea is substantial, with hot meat pies, potted meat, cheese dishes, lots of cakes, and sometimes stewed fruit and cream. It is a meal one looks forward to all day.

Afternoon tea and high tea would not be worthwhile without the star of the table—the tea pot. At 4 P.M. tea is usually served in a silver service and at high tea in a big china tea pot with a hand-knitted cosy to keep it hot. Indian tea is used most frequently but everyone has a special blend. When I was a girl, the grocer would blend tea to suit one's taste. Grannie also had several caddies filled with different teas, and she'd mix a bit of this and that to make her own blend. Tea should suit the water in which it is brewed: hard water is best for the rich Ceylon teas, and soft water improves the taste of the lighter teas, such as jasmine and the green teas, which one can drink without sugar or milk. Try experimenting with different teas to

find which one you like best. Make a friend of the teapot.

Country Host has a large assortment of teas. Most of the time I use loose teas from cannisters. I measure out one spoonful of tea per person and an extra one for the pot. First the pot should be warmed with hot water, then emptied. Put in the tea and add enough boiling water to cover the tea leaves. I let it stand, with the lid on, for 3 to 5 minutes to brew the tea. Then fill up the pot with more boiling water. For a good cup of tea put sugar and milk into the cup first, and then pour in the hot tea. It really does make a difference.

Earl Grey is my very favorite tea. It's so fragrant, I have even considered putting it into sachets just as I would with lavender. My family thinks that idea is a bit peculiar, however.

I also love Keemun, a black tea from Taiwan (formerly Formosa), which turns burgundy-colored when brewed. Assam tea is a wonderful Indian tea, similar to the tea we used when I was a child. Ceylon Breakfast is another excellent full-flavored tea. Ch'a Ching tea, served in Chinese restaurants, is one I like to drink plain. Imperial Gunpowder is a green tea and it is absolutely delicious as iced tea with sprigs of fresh mint leaves. For a smoky-flavored tea, there is none more vigorous than Lapsang Souchong. Then there are the spiced teas: nutmeg and cinnamon; lemon tea with tiny pieces of lemon peel; mint tea all ready to become a fragrant drink, and the exotic-sounding jasmine tea.

The herb teas one can buy today are becoming very popular. Country Host has several of these on its shelves. Some are described as helpful for a good night's sleep, soothing to the tummy, or just plain nice to the taste buds. Most important to some people, they do not have tannic acid. My favorite among herb teas is Hibiscus. It tastes like a fruit wine and turns a rich brown-red color when brewed. I drink it with a teaspoon of honey. There are others to choose from such as camomile, peppermint, rose hips, alfalfa-mint, comfrey, papaya-mint and summer meadow blend.

I have often thought that tea-tasting parties would make a nice change from wine-tasting parties. A good cup of tea is certainly akin to a good glass of wine. I would have an array of pretty teapots—china ones for the Indian and China teas, and the old-fashioned brown earthenware pots for the Earl Grey and Ceylon Breakfast. The spice teas could be set on a tray in their teabags and brewed right in the cup from a supply of boiling water. I would serve tea breads with the Indian and China teas, buttered scones with the Earl Grey and Ceylon teas and Shrewsbury biscuits and delicate butter cookies with the spice teas.

Depending upon the weather, an English man or woman will say, "Let's have a cup of tea to cool off," or "Let's have a cup of tea to warm ourselves." To celebrate a meeting, they'll say "Come on home and I'll put the kettle on for a cup of tea." And, of course, when one is sad, "Let's have a cup of tea together and perk up!" One chooses tea to complement the life one leads.

I have a sweet tooth. The habit of having a cup of tea many times a day with a biscuit or cookie is not for the calorie-conscious. However, one may indulge oneself from time to time—and I do.

Country Host has a selection of cookies that are plain and old-fashioned in content, such as oatmeal, chocolate chip, cinnamon sugar, shortbread, and currant biscuit. At holiday times we make gingerbread boys and girls, fudge, rumballs, and other treats. Making cookies takes time and patience. For the holidays a day should be devoted to getting the ingredients together and planning exactly which recipes will be used. During busy times my assistant, Debbie, has the infinite patience to keep cookie sheets filled and ready for the oven. We work ahead and have batches of cookie dough ready to be dropped by spoonfuls onto cookie sheets or rolled out to be cut into different shapes. Once a cookie making session is on, we can't afford to let the ovens cool off, so extra hands are a boon. Seeing glass jars filled with homemade cookies is a delight to me. Fudge, toffee apples, and candies are not too difficult a task. It is so nice to make a gift of one's handiwork. Homemade sweets of any kind, wrapped and beribboned as gifts, are a real labor of love and much appreciated by the receiver.

Cake baking comes under the heading of gifts of love, too. Fruit cake is a sentimental favorite, especially at Christmas, because it keeps so well. Lighter cakes like ginger and carrot are ideal as hostess gifts. It isn't such a big job to whip up a fragrant lemon cake for a thoughtful present. It is very easy to please a family with children by taking a box of pretty cupcakes. Make any of the light cake recipes, line muffin tins with cupcake papers, and decorate the cakes to suit the tastes of the audience.

We no longer rely upon bread as a primary source of nutrients. Long considered the staff of life, we have access to more balanced diets today. Most of us eat bread in some form every day of our lives. My bread collection incudes sweet breads, buns, crumpets, muffins, and scones. Water biscuits and Scottish oatcakes are descendants of hard flat breads. Sweet biscuits, or cookies, are made today with enriched flours, but they developed from the basic concept of bread—yeast, flour and water, plus sweet ingredients and eggs. Today baking powder and baking soda are used as leavening agents for the sweeter breads.

The smell of homemade bread baking is superb—what a pity we can't bottle it! Tea time means all of these recipes to me, from thinly sliced and buttered bread to scones and crumpets oozing with butter and jam.

Eccles Cakes

4 TABLESPOONS BUTTER

¼ CUP BROWN SUGAR

½ CUP RAISINS

½ CUP CURRANTS

½ CUP CANDIED FRUIT PEEL,

JUICE AND GRATED RIND OF 1 LEMON OR 2 TABLESPOONS MADEIRA

¼ TEASPOON ALLSPICE

½ RECIPE PUFF PASTRY (PAGE 196)

MILK

GRANULATED SUGAR

Cream butter and brown sugar. Mix in raisins, currants, fruit peel, lemon or Madiera, allspice. Roll out puff pastry to 1/8-inch thickness. Cut into twelve 4-inch rounds. Brush edges of rounds with milk.

Place a spoonful of the mixture into the center of each circle. Pinch edges to cover filling completely. Twist to enclose. Turn over and press with fingers to flatten into a circle and to evenly distribute filling. Make two slits on each cake. Brush with milk and sprinkle with granulated sugar. Place on greased baking sheets lined with waxed paper. Bake at 400°F. for 25 to 30 minutes, or until puffed golden brown. Cool.

YIELD: 12 CAKES

Coconut Pyramids

Coconut pyramids were our first accomplishment in cooking class when I went to school.

8 OUNCES FINE DRIED COCONUT

½ CUP GRANULATED SUGAR

2 LARGE EGG WHITES,
BEATEN

GLACÉ CHERRIES

Mix coconut and sugar. Add egg whites and mix to a moist consistency . Line a cookie sheet with buttered wax paper. Fill an egg cup or other small mold with mixture, invert onto cookie sheet, and place a piece of glacé cherry on top of each pyramid. Bake in a 350°F. oven for 15 to 20 minutes, or until golden brown.

YIELD: APPROXIMATELY 12,
DEPENDING ON SIZE OF MOLD

Rock Cakes

2 CUPS ALL-PURPOSE FLOUR

2½ TEASPOONS BAKING POWDER

10 TABLESPOONS BUTTER

2/3 CUP SUGAR

½ CUP CURRANTS

½ CUP RAISINS

¼ CUP CANDIED PEELS

1 EGG,
WELL BEATEN

MILK

SUGAR

Sift flour and baking powder together. Rub in butter until mixture resembles coarse bread crumbs. Mix in sugar. Add dried fruits and candied peels. Add egg and just enough milk to make a stiff dough. Do not make mixture too soft—the cakes will spread. Grease and lightly flour a baking sheet. Place heaping tablespoons of mixture about 2 inches apart on baking sheet. Sprinkle with a little sugar. Bake for 10 to 12 minutes in top part of a 450°F. oven. If tops brown too quickly, lower heat to 400°F. after 5 minutes. Serve warm or cold.

YIELD: 18 CAKES

Queen Cakes or Queenies

8 TABLESPOONS BUTTER

½ CUP SUGAR

3 EGGS

1½ CUPS ALL-PURPOSE FLOUR

½ TEASPOON BAKING POWDER

PINCH OF SALT

½ CUP RAISINS

GRATED RIND OF 1 LEMON

CANDIED PEEL

Butter small cupcake tins.

Cream together butter and sugar. Add eggs one at a time, beating well after each addition.

Sift together flour, baking powder, and salt. Add to egg mixture and stir. Mix in raisins and grated rind. Fill each of cupcake tins half full of the mixture. Decorate tops with pieces of candied peel.

Bake in a 375°F. oven for 15 to 20 minutes. Cool.

YIELD: 12 CUPCAKES

Carrot Cake

This is best if baked a day before serving.

3 CUPS ALL-PURPOSE FLOUR

1 TEASPOON CINNAMON

2 TEASPOONS BAKING POWDER

2 TEASPOONS BAKING SODA

1 TEASPOON SALT

2 CUPS SUGAR

1 1/3 CUPS VEGETABLE OIL

4 EGGS

2 CUPS CARROTS (ABOUT 6 MEDIUM-SIZED CARROTS), FINELY GRATED

1 CUP WALNUTS, CHOPPED

Sift together flour, cinnamon, baking powder, soda, and salt.

In another bowl, mix sugar with oil and beat well with electric mixer. Add ¼ of flour mixture to sugar and oil, then beat in one egg. Alternate flour and eggs, beating well. Add carrots and nuts. Mix well. Place mixture in lightly greased tube pan or divide into greased loaf pans.

Bake in a 350° oven for 1 hour if using tube pan, or 40 to 45 minutes for loaf pans. When top of cake is firm, remove from oven. Cool on wire racks.

YIELD: A 9-INCH TUBE CAKE OR
6 EIGHT-OUNCE LOAVES

Lemon Cake

1½ CUPS BUTTER

3 CUPS SUGAR

6 EGGS

3¾ CUPS ALL-PURPOSE FLOUR

1 TABLESPOON BAKING POWDER

½ TEASPOON SALT

1½ CUPS MILK

GRATED RIND AND JUICE OF
3 LEMONS

1 TABLESPOON SUGAR

Cream butter and sugar. Add eggs and beat until creamy. Sift together flour, baking powder, and salt. Add to creamed mixture, alternating with the milk. Add lemon rind. Mix well again.

Butter and flour baking tins, then fill with batter. Bake until golden brown in a 350°F. oven for 45 minutes for small tins or 1 hour and 5 minutes for large tin. Cool cakes slightly and prick tops with a fork. Dissolve sugar in lemon juice and heat. Brush over tops of cakes.

YIELD: A 10-INCH TUBE CAKE OR
7 EIGHT-OUNCE LOAVES

Cider Cake

This is a moist cake with a decidedly apple flavor.

2 EGGS,
AT ROOM TEMPERATURE

8 TABLESPOONS BUTTER

½ CUP SUGAR

2 CUPS ALL-PURPOSE FLOUR

1 TEASPOON BAKING POWDER

1 TEASPOON NUTMEG

5 OUNCES CIDER

Beat eggs over a pan of warm water. Cream butter and sugar. Add eggs, mixing thoroughly. Sift flour and baking powder together. Fold into egg-and-butter mixture. Add nutmeg and cider. Mix well.

Spoon the mixture into a 9-inch cake pan lined with buttered wax paper. Bake in a 375°F. oven for 20 minutes, or until the top springs back when gently pressed.

YIELD: A 9-INCH CAKE

Seed Cake

This cake is best when made several days ahead of time.

1 POUND BUTTER

1 POUND SUGAR

9 EGGS

1 POUND ALL-PURPOSE FLOUR

1 TEASPOON GRATED NUTMEG

1 TEASPOON CINNAMON

2 TABLESPOONS CARAWAY SEEDS

Cream butter and sugar together until fluffy.

Beat the eggs in a bowl set over a pan of hot water. Stir flour, nutmeg and cinnamon together and add caraway seeds. Fold flour mixture into creamed mixture.

Line a 10-inch round cake pan with wax paper and grease it. Turn mixture into pan, smooth the top and bake in a 350°F. oven for 2 hours.

Seed cake keeps very well if unused portion is wrapped in foil and stored in a cool place.

YIELD: A 10-INCH ROUND CAKE

Sponge Cake

6 EGGS,
SEPARATED

1½ CUPS SUGAR

1½ CUPS ALL-PURPOSE FLOUR
SIFTED

1 TEASPOON BAKING POWDER

¼ TEASPOON SALT

1/3 CUP WATER

2 TEASPOONS VANILLA EXTRACT

1 TEASPOON LEMON JUICE

1 TEASPOON LEMON PEEL,
GRATED

½ TEASPOON CREAM OF TARTAR

CONFECTIONER'S SUGAR

Beat egg yolks until thick and lemon colored. Gradually add sugar, mixing well. Sift together flour, baking powder, and salt. Alternate adding dry ingredients with water, vanilla, lemon juice, and peel. Stir until just blended.

Beat egg whites with cream of tartar until stiff. Fold gently into batter. Pour into an ungreased 10-inch tube pan. Bake in 325°F. oven for 55 to 60 minutes. Cool in pan before removing. Sprinkle with confectioner's sugar.

YIELD: A 10-INCH TUBE CAKE

Victoria Sponge Cake

A simple, delightful cake.

2 CUPS ALL-PURPOSE FLOUR

2 TEASPOONS BAKING POWDER

1 CUP BUTTER

1 CUP SUGAR

4 EGGS,
WELL BEATEN

RASPBERRY JAM

CONFECTIONER'S SUGAR

Sift flour and baking powder together.

Cream butter and sugar. Alternate additions of flour and egg, beating well after each addition. Divide mixture between two greased and floured 8-inch pans. Bake in center of a preheated 375°F. oven for 25 minutes, or until tops spring back when lightly pressed. Cool, then remove from pans.

Cover bottom layer with raspberry jam, then set other layer in place. Dust with confectioner's sugar.

YIELD: AN 8-INCH CAKE

Madeira Cake

Named as an accompaniment for a glass of Madeira.

¾ CUP BUTTER

¾ CUP SUGAR

2 CUPS ALL-PURPOSE FLOUR

2 TEASPOONS BAKING POWDER

3 EGGS,
WELL BEATEN

1 TEASPOON LEMON PEEL,
GRATED

2 TO 3 TABLESPOONS MILK

SUGAR

CANDIED LEMON PEEL

Cream butter and sugar together. Sift together flour and baking powder. Alternately add eggs and flour to the butter-sugar mixture. Blend well after each addition. Mix in enough milk to make a nice dropping consistency. Spoon batter into a greased and floured 7-inch cake pan or loaf tin. Sprinkle a little granulated sugar on cake and decorate with pieces of candied lemon peel. Bake for 1¼ hours in a preheated 375°F. oven. Test for doneness by inserting a metal skewer into cake. If skewer comes out clean, the cake is done. Cool in cake pan.

YIELD: A 7-INCH ROUND OR
LOAF CAKE

Yorkshire Parkin

This cake is similar in taste to ginger cake, but the texture is somewhat heavier due to the oatmeal. For a hearty cake to have with tea or coffee or as an afternoon snack, there is nothing better.

5 CUPS QUICK-COOKING OATMEAL

1 CUP ALL-PURPOSE FLOUR

2 TEASPOONS GROUND GINGER

2 CUPS MOLASSES

¾ CUP BUTTER

¼ CUP SUGAR

½ TEASPOON BAKING SODA

1 TEASPOON WARM MILK

Combine oatmeal, flour, and ginger in a large bowl. Make a well in the center. Set aside.

Combine molasses, butter, and sugar in the top of a double boiler, stirring until softened. Pour molasses mixture into the well in oatmeal mixture. Blend together. Combine baking soda with milk, then stir into mixture. Spoon into a well-buttered 9x12x3-inch baking pan. Bake in a preheated 325°F. oven for 1 hour, or until the parkin is firm to the touch. Cool in the baking pan for a few days. This cake sets hard while cooling, but becomes moist and soft if kept for several days before eating.

YIELD: A 9x12-INCH CAKE

Ginger Cake

2 CUPS ALL-PURPOSE FLOUR

½ TEASPOON GROUND CLOVES

1 TEASPOON CINNAMON

½ TEASPOON GINGER

½ TEASPOON SALT

1 CUP SUGAR

½ CUP BUTTER

1 TEASPOON BAKING SODA

1 CUP BOILING WATER

1 EGG,
BEATEN

½ CUP MOLASSES

Sift dry ingredients together into a bowl. Add butter to boiling water and stir until melted. Add to dry ingredients, then mix in egg and molasses. Pour mixture into greased pans. Bake in a 350°F. oven for 45 to 50 minutes.

YIELD: A 10-INCH ROUND OR
8 SMALL CAKES

Chocolate Swiss Roll

9 TABLESPOONS CAKE FLOUR

9 TABLESPOONS COCOA

¾ TEASPOON BAKING POWDER

½ TEASPOON SALT

6 EGGS,
SEPARATED

1 CUP PLUS 1 TABLESPOON SUGAR

1½ TEASPOONS VANILLA

CONFECTIONER'S SUGAR

1 PINT HEAVY CREAM

Sift flour, cocoa, baking powder, and salt together *three times.* Beat egg whites until stiff and gradually fold in sugar. Beat yolks until lemon colored, then add vanilla. Fold yolks into whites. Fold in flour mixture.

Line a 9x14x1-inch pan with buttered wax paper. Pour mixture into pan, spreading evenly. Bake in a preheated 400°F. oven for 12 minutes. Turn out on a kitchen towel dusted with confectioner's sugar. Remove wax paper and trim any crisp edges. Gently lift edge of towel and fold cake as for a jelly roll. Cool.

Beat cream until stiff. Carefully unroll cake and spread with whipped cream. Roll up again and sprinkle with more confectioner's sugar. Refrigerate until served.

6 SERVINGS

Chocolate Cake

Chocolate butter icing (page 193) can be used, but the cake is rich enough without it.

1 CUP BUTTER

1 CUP SUGAR

7 EGGS,
SEPARATED

8 OUNCES BITTER CHOCOLATE,
GRATED

8 OUNCES SLIVERED ALMONDS

1 CUP ALL-PURPOSE FLOUR,
SIFTED

¼ TEASPOON SALT

Cream butter and sugar together. Add beaten egg yolks and mix well. Add chocolate, almonds, and salt. Mix again. Beat egg whites until stiff. Alternate adding egg whites with flour to the mixture. Blend thoroughly. Grease an 8x4-inch round cake pan, then line with greased wax paper. Pour batter into cake pan and bake in a 325°F. oven for about 1½ hours, or until cake is firm to the touch. Cool cake in pan, then cool on rack.

YIELD: AN 8-INCH ROUND CAKE

Dundee Cake

This medium-dark cake is excellent for any special occasion. For an English wedding cake, bake the fruit cake several weeks ahead of time and douse the cake at least once a week with brandy. Before decorating, brush the top and sides with apricot jam and then cover with a layer of almond paste (page 191). Let dry for 1 or 2 days, then apply the white royal icing (page 192) and decorate.

¾ CUPS BUTTER

¾ CUPS BROWN SUGAR,
PACKED DOWN

3 EGGS,
WELL BEATEN

1½ TEASPOONS BAKING POWDER

2 CUPS ALL-PURPOSE FLOUR

1 POUND MIXED DRIED FRUIT
(RAISINS, CURRANTS, AND DATES)

2 OUNCES ALMONDS,
CHOPPED

2 OUNCES SLIVERED ALMONDS

2 OUNCES GLACÉ CHERRIES

2 OUNCES CANDIED PEEL

2 TABLESPOONS MILK
(APPROXIMATELY)

1 TABLESPOON MOLASSES

1 TEASPOON ALLSPICE

1 EGG WHITE,
BEATEN

In first bowl cream butter and sugar. Add eggs and mix well.

Reserving 1 tablespoon flour, sift remaining flour, baking powder, and allspice into another bowl.

Mix dried fruit, chopped almonds, cherries and candied peels. Sprinkle with 1 tablespoon of flour and mix lightly.

Stir dry ingredients into creamed mixture. Add molasses and just enough milk to make a slow dropping consistency. Add fruit mixture and blend well. Turn mixture into a greased and floured 8x3-inch cake pan. Decorate outer edge of cake with slivered almonds. Brush egg white over top of cake. Bake in a preheated 325°F. oven for 2 to 2¼ hours. Cool slightly in pan before turning onto a wire rack.

8 TO 10 SERVINGS

Christmas Cake

Best when made 3 or 4 weeks before Christmas.

3 CUPS PLUS 1 TABLESPOON ALL-PURPOSE FLOUR

1 TEASPOON CINNAMON

1 TEASPOON ALLSPICE

½ TEASPOON SALT

1 CUP BUTTER

1 CUP BROWN SUGAR

4 EGGS,
BEATEN

1 POUND CURRANTS

8 OUNCES RAISINS

8 OUNCES SULTANAS OR DATES,
CHOPPED

4 OUNCES CANDIED PEEL

4 OUNCES GLACÉ CHERRIES

4 OUNCES BLANCHED ALMONDS

4 TABLESPOONS BRANDY

GRATED RIND OF LEMON

1 TABLESPOON MOLASSES

Line cake tin with a double thickness of wax paper and butter paper generously. Tie a band of brown paper that rises 3 inches above the outside of the pan. Sift 3 cups flour, spices, and salt together. Cream sugar and butter together. Add beaten eggs and mix well.

Mix dried fruits, candied peel, glacé cherries, and almonds. Sprinkle with 1 tablespoon flour and mix lightly.

Combine dry ingredients with creamed ingredients. Add brandy, lemon rind, and molasses. Add dried fruit and mix well. Turn into prepared cake pan. Bake in a preheated 325°F. oven for 1½ hours, then reduce to 275°F. and continue baking for another 1¾ to 2 hours longer. Cool in cake pan.

Remove paper and wrap cake in cheese cloth, then store in an airtight tin for 3 or 4 weeks. Each week sprinkle cake with brandy, then rewrap and keep in tin until time for icing. Four or five days before Christmas, apply almond paste (page 191). Let dry 1 or 2 days and then apply royal icing (page 192). Decorate with holly sprigs.

YIELD: A 9-INCH ROUND OR
8-INCH SQUARE CAKE

Apple Cake

This cake is moist and keeps well in the refrigerator for 2 weeks. It is delicious hot or cold.

2 EGGS

¾ CUP BROWN SUGAR

½ CUP CORN OIL

1 TEASPOON VANILLA EXTRACT

3 CUPS APPLES,
DICED

1¾ CUPS ALL-PURPOSE FLOUR

½ TEASPOON SALT

1 TEASPOON BAKING SODA

½ TEASPOON CINNAMON

½ TEASPOON NUTMEG

Combine eggs and brown sugar. Mix in oil, vanilla, and apples.

Sift together flour, baking soda, salt, and spices. Fold into the apple mixture and blend thoroughly.

Pour mixture into a greased and floured 9x9-inch pan. Bake in a 350°F. oven for 35 minutes, or until top springs back when gently pressed.

YIELD: 9 LARGE SQUARES

Country Host Apple Pie

REGULAR SHORTCRUST PASTRY
(PAGE 195)

8 TO 9 MEDIUM-SIZED TART APPLES,
PEELED, CORED, AND SLICED

1 TABLESPOON FLOUR

¾ CUP SUGAR

1 TABLESPOON BUTTER

1 TEASPOON CINNAMON

1 EGG,
BEATEN WITH 2 TEASPOONS WATER

Divide pastry in half and roll out to fit a pie pan. Line pan with pastry. Cover with apples. Sprinkle with flour and sugar, reserving 1 teaspoon. Dot apples with butter and sprinkle with cinnamon. Cover with remaining pastry. Trim and turn the edges under to seal, crimping with thumbs or tines of a fork. Make two small slits on top and brush the crust with egg. Sprinkle with sugar. Bake in a 350°F. oven for 1¼ hours, or until golden. For your first pie it might be easier to mix the apples with sugar, flour, and cinnamon before putting the mixture into the pie shell.

6 SERVINGS

Mama's Strudel

2 CUPS ALL-PURPOSE FLOUR

¼ TEASPOON SALT

1 EGG,
BEATEN

1/3 CUP WARM WATER

10 TABLESPOONS BUTTER,
MELTED

CONFECTIONER'S SUGAR

Sift flour and salt into a bowl. Add egg and gradually add warm water. Mix well. Add 2 tablespoons butter. Knead dough in bowl for about 20 minutes until dough is smooth and elastic and does not stick to the bowl or fingers. Place dough in the center of a large table that has been covered with a floured cloth. Cover the dough with the mixing bowl and let stand for 20 to 30 minutes. While dough is resting, prepare the filling (recipe follows).

Begin to stretch dough. Take a rolling pin and roll out the dough to a large circle. Brush top generously with melted butter. Begin stretching with hands from underside of pastry. Pull very gently and stretch until dough covers table completely. Dough should be paper thin—it requires patience. When this is done, let dough dry for 5 minutes. Spread with filling and sprinkle evenly with 6 to 8 tablespoons of melted butter. Hold up two ends of the floured cloth and gently roll up the strudel. Place seam side down on a greased baking sheet. Bake for 30 to 35 minutes in a 400°F. oven. Sprinkle with confectioner's sugar.

8 SERVINGS

Filling

4 POUNDS TART APPLES,
PEELED, CORED AND THINLY SLICED

1 CUP RAISINS

1½ CUPS SUGAR

½ CUP WALNUTS OR PECANS,
CHOPPED

½ CUP BREAD CRUMBS

Combine all ingredients and mix well.

Apple Flan

A flan is similar to a pie, except the pastry covers a 9-inch ring and less fruit is used because the top is flat.

½ RECIPE FOR REGULAR
SHORTCRUST PASTRY (PAGE 195)

4 MEDIUM APPLES,
PEELED, CORED, AND SLICED

½ CUP SUGAR

1 TABLESPOON FRESH LEMON JUICE

1 TABLESPOON BUTTER

1 EGG,
LIGHTLY BEATEN

Set a flan ring on a baking sheet. Roll out 2/3 of the pastry and line the ring. Place apples flat on the pastry. Sprinkle with sugar and lemon juice, dot with butter and trim the edges.

Roll out remaining pastry. Cut into eight ¾-inch strips. Set the strips across the apples in lattice fashion, and brush with egg. Sprinkle generously with sugar. Bake in a 425°F. oven for 10 minutes, then reduce heat to 350°F. for 35 minutes. Serve warm or cold with heavy cream.

6 SERVINGS

Treacle Tart

½ RECIPE FOR REGULAR
SHORTCRUST PASTRY (PAGE 195)

4 OUNCES FRESH BREAD CRUMBS

1 CUP LYLE'S GOLDEN SYRUP
(AVAILABLE IN SPECIALTY
FOOD SHOPS)

2 TABLESPOONS BUTTER

JUICE AND GRATED RIND OF
2 LEMONS

HEAVY CREAM

Roll out pastry to fit an 8-inch pie pan. Save leftover pastry for lattice strips. Crimp the edges of the pastry with fork tines or fingers.

Put syrup and butter into a double boiler and heat until runny. Add lemon juice, rind, and bread crumbs. Stir until well mixed. Pour filling into pastry shell. Make lattice work design with pastry pieces.

Bake in a 350°F. oven for 40 to 45 minutes until pastry is lightly browned. Serve warm with heavy cream.

6 SERVINGS

Bakewell Tart

½ RECIPE FOR REGULAR
SHORTCRUST PASTRY (PAGE 195)

RASPBERRY JAM

6 TABLESPOONS BUTTER

4 TABLESPOONS SUGAR

2 EGGS,
WELL BEATEN

2 TABLESPOONS RICE FLOUR

PINCH OF SALT

1 TEASPOON ALMOND EXTRACT

Prepare pastry and roll out to fit an 8-inch tart pan. Spread a generous amount of raspberry jam on the bottom of tart shell.

Cream butter and sugar. Alternately add beaten eggs and rice flour. Mix in salt and extract. Pour filling into tart shell.

Bake in a 400°F. oven for 40 to 45 minutes. After 25 minutes cover tart with wax paper or foil to prevent too much browning. Serve warm.

8 SERVINGS

Lemon Curd Tartlets

CRISPY SHORTCRUST
PASTRY (PAGE 196)

GRATED RIND AND JUICE OF
3 LARGE LEMONS

3 EGGS PLUS 2 YOLKS

4 TABLESPOONS BUTTER

2 CUPS SUGAR (3 CUPS FOR
A SWEETER CURD)

Prepare the pastry, baking 50 tartlet shells.

Place lemon rind and juice in top of a double boiler. Beat eggs until thick and lemon colored, adding sugar gradually. Add to lemon juice and rind. Over slow to moderate heat, stir lemon mixture, adding butter a little at a time. Let pieces melt before adding the next. Cook, stirring frequently, until curd is thick and creamy. Refrigerate. This quantity is enough for 50 shells using ½ teaspoon of curd for each tart.

YIELD: 50 TARTLETS

Apple Curd Tartlets

Make this in small quantities—it is best when fresh.

CRISPY SHORTCRUST
PASTRY (PAGE 196)

2 POUNDS APPLES, CORED
AND QUARTERED

½ CUP WATER

1 CUP BUTTER

1 CUP SUGAR

2 EGGS,
BEATEN

JUICE AND RIND OF 1 LEMON

Prepare the pastry, baking 50 tartlet shells.

Cook apples in water until soft. Force the pulp through a sieve and discard the remaining peels. Place sugar in a double boiler with butter, eggs, lemon juice, and rind. Mix and stir until sugar is dissolved. Add the apples. Continue cooking and stirring often, until curd thickens. Refrigerate.

Spoon ½ teaspoon curd into tartlet shells and serve.

YIELD: 50 TARTLETS

Baked Custard Tart

½ RECIPE FOR REGULAR
SHORTCRUST PASTRY (PAGE 195)

1 TABLESPOON RASPBERRY JAM

1½ CUPS MILK

2 EGGS

2½ TABLESPOONS SUGAR

1 TEASPOON VANILLA EXTRACT

1 TEASPOON BUTTER

PINCH OF SALT

NUTMEG

Line 9-inch pan with pastry and bake in a 425°F. oven for 10 minutes. Put a piece of wax paper or aluminum foil in pastry shell and weigh down with rice or dried beans to keep pastry from puffing while baking. Remove from oven and discard paper and beans.

Spread jam on bottom of partially cooked shell.

Warm the milk. Beat eggs, sugar, salt, and vanilla together. Pour milk into egg mixture, stirring while pouring. Pour mixture into pastry shell. Cut butter into little pieces and place on top. Sprinkle with nutmeg.

Bake in a 400°F. oven for 40 minutes, or until custard is just set. Remove from oven and cool. Serve warm or cold.

6 TO 8 SERVINGS

Chewy Oatmeal Cookies

1 CUP ALL-PURPOSE FLOUR, SIFTED

½ TEASPOON SALT

¾ TEASPOON BAKING SODA

1 TEASPOON CINNAMON

¼ TEASPOON NUTMEG

¾ CUP BUTTER,
SOFTENED

1 1/3 CUPS BROWN SUGAR,
FIRMLY PACKED

2 EGGS

1 TEASPOON VANILLA

2 CUPS QUICK-COOKING OATS

1 CUP RAISINS

Sift together flour, salt, baking soda, and spices. Add butter, sugar, eggs, and vanilla. Beat until smooth, about 2 minutes. Stir in oats and raisins. Drop heaping teaspoons onto a greased baking sheet. Bake in a preheated 350°F. oven for 12 to 15 minutes.

YIELD: 3½ DOZEN

Cinnamon Sugar Cookies

1½ CUPS SWEET BUTTER

2 CUPS CONFECTIONER'S SUGAR

2 EGG YOLKS

4 CUPS ALL-PURPOSE FLOUR,
SIFTED

¼ CUP SUGAR

½ TEASPOON CINNAMON

Cream butter and sugar until light and fluffy. Add egg yolks, mixing well. Blend in flour and shape into a ball. Roll out 1/3 of the dough at a time on a lightly floured board to a thickness between 1/8- and 1/4-inch. Cut rounds with a 3-inch cookie cutter. Combine sugar and cinnamon, then sprinkle in the center of each cookie. Bake on ungreased baking sheets in a 350°F. oven for about 10 minutes. These cookies brown quickly, so check once or twice. Cool on cookie sheets.

YIELD: 4 DOZEN

Shortbread

8 TABLESPOONS LIGHTLY SALTED
BUTTER

¼ CUP SUGAR

¼ CUP FINE SEMOLINA

1 CUP ALL-PURPOSE FLOUR

Cream butter and sugar. Add semolina and flour. Mix together and knead to a smooth consistency. Press dough into a 9-inch pie pan. Bake in a 325°F. oven for 20 to 25 minutes until golden. Cut into 8 or 10 wedges while still warm. Cool and store in airtight tin.

NOTE: For decoration, press dough around edge of pie pan with fork tines. Take a pastry wheel and mark out the portions before baking. This makes an ideal gift left in the pie pan, wrapped with colored cellophane paper and tied with ribbon.

YIELD: 8 TO 10 WEDGES

Seed Cookies

½ CUP SWEET BUTTER

1 CUP SUGAR

¼ CUP WATER

2 EGGS,
WELL BEATEN

3 CUPS ALL-PURPOSE FLOUR

2 TEASPOONS BAKING POWDER

2 TEASPOONS CARAWAY SEEDS

Cream butter and sugar. Add water and eggs, mixing well. Sift flour and baking powder together. Combine with butter mixture. Add caraway seeds and mix again. Gather dough into a ball. Roll out half of the dough to 1/8-inch thick, on a lightly floured board. Cut into rounds with a 3-inch cookie cutter. Place on lightly buttered baking sheet. Bake 10 minutes in a 350°F. oven, or until lightly browned.

YIELD: 3 DOZEN

Ginger Biscuits

1 CUP DARK MOLASSES

2 CUPS BROWN SUGAR

1 CUP BUTTER

1 TEASPOON BAKING SODA

1 HEAPING TEASPOON GINGER

½ TEASPOON CINNAMON

2 EGGS,
WELL BEATEN

3½ TO 4 CUPS ALL-PURPOSE FLOUR,
SIFTED

Put molasses, sugar, and butter into a saucepan. Bring to the boiling point. Pour mixture into a large bowl containing baking soda that has been dissolved in a little water. Add spices, eggs, and flour. Mix well with a spoon. Let mixture cool.

Roll out thinly on lightly floured board. Cut into rounds with a 3-inch cookie cutter. Bake on ungreased cookie sheets in a 325°F. oven for 15 to 20 minutes until golden brown. Cool slightly before removing from cookie sheets.

YIELD: 4 DOZEN

Crisps

½ CUP BUTTER,
MELTED

1 CUP SUGAR

1½ CUPS DARK MOLASSES

3 CUPS ALL-PURPOSE FLOUR,
SIFTED

Thoroughly mix butter into sugar, molasses, and flour. Drop by teaspoonfuls about 4 inches apart onto greased cookie sheets. Bake in a 325°F. oven until firm and light brown, about 15 to 20 minutes. Remove from cookie sheet with a broad bladed knife and quickly place over the edge of a bowl to curl while cooling.

YIELD: 3½ DOZEN

Coconut Drops

2 CUPS ALL-PURPOSE FLOUR

1½ TEASPOONS BAKING POWDER

½ CUP BUTTER

½ TEASPOON SALT

¾ CUP COCONUT
GRATED

¾ CUP SUGAR

1 EGG,
WELL BEATEN

2/3 CUP MILK

Sift together flour, baking powder, and salt. Rub in butter. Add sugar and coconut. Stir in the milk and egg, mixing to a stiff dough. Drop by the teaspoonful onto a lightly greased cookie sheet. Bake 15 minutes in a 375°F. oven until golden brown.

YIELD: 3 DOZEN

Walnut Drops

¼ CUP BUTTER

½ CUP SUGAR

2 EGGS,
WELL BEATEN

1/3 CUP MILK

¼ CUP WALNUTS,
FINELY CHOPPED

1½ CUPS ALL-PURPOSE FLOUR

1½ TEASPOONS BAKING POWDER

½ TEASPOON SALT

Cream butter and sugar. Add eggs, milk, and nuts, mixing well. Sift together flour, baking powder, and salt. Add to butter mixture. Mix well. Drop by the teaspoonful onto greased cookie sheets. Bake in a 325°F. oven for 10 to 15 minutes until golden brown.

NOTE: Pecans or macadamia nuts can be substituted for walnuts.

YIELD: 30 COOKIES

Almond Wafers

½ CUP BUTTER

1 CUP SUGAR

1 EGG

1 TEASPOON ALMOND EXTRACT

½ CUP WHOLE ALMONDS,
FINELY GROUND

GRATED RIND OF 1 LEMON

1½ TEASPOONS OF ALLSPICE

2 CUPS ALL-PURPOSE FLOUR,
SIFTED

Cream butter and sugar. Beat in egg, lemon rind, extract and almonds. Add allspice to flour and sift again. Add flour to butter-sugar mixture, mixing well. Form into a roll and refrigerate overnight. Cut into thin slices and place on cookie sheets. Bake in a 325° F. oven for 20 minutes, or until light brown.

YIELD: QUANTITY DEPENDS
ON DIAMETER OF THE ROLL
OF DOUGH

Nut Crescents

2 CUPS FLOUR,
SIFTED

½ CUP SUGAR

1 CUP BUTTER

8 OUNCES FILBERTS,
GROUND

1 TEASPOON VANILLA

CONFECTIONER'S SUGAR

Cream butter and sugar. Slowly mix in flour. Add nuts and vanilla. Mix well and form into a ball. Roll out to ¼-inch thickness on a floured board. Cut into 2-inch squares. Roll from one corner to the opposite corner and shape into a crescent. Bake on greased cookie sheets for 15 minutes in a 400°F. oven. Cool and dust with confectioner's sugar.

YIELD: 3 DOZEN

Christmas Butter Cookies

2 CUPS BUTTER

1 CUP VEGETABLE SHORTENING

1 CUP SUGAR

5 CUPS FLOUR,
SIFTED 3 TIMES

8 EGG YOLKS,
LIGHTLY BEATEN

2 TEASPOONS VANILLA

3 TABLESPOONS LEMON JUICE

1 EGG WHITE,
BEATEN

COLORED SPRINKLES, SUGAR, OR
CHOPPED NUTS (OPTIONAL)

Cream butter and shortening. Add sugar and cream until smooth. Gradually add flour and mix with pastry blender until mixture is the size of peas. Add egg yolks, vanilla, and lemon juice. Mix dough lightly and divide in half. Roll out one half at a time to ¼-inch thick. Cut shapes with Christmas cookie cutters and place on lightly buttered cookie sheets. Brush tops with a little beaten egg white. Sprinkle tops with colored sprinkles, colored sugar, or chopped nuts. Bake in a 350°F. oven for 12 minutes until edges are delicate brown.

YIELD: 7 TO 8 DOZEN

Apricot Bars

This recipe was given to me a few years ago by two young people named Julie and Phillip. It has become a favorite Country Host dessert. The bars will keep in an airtight tin for 3 to 4 weeks.

1¼ CUPS DRIED APRICOTS,
CHOPPED

1 CUP SWEET BUTTER,
SOFTENED

½ CUP SUGAR

2½ CUPS ALL-PURPOSE FLOUR

1 TEASPOON BAKING POWDER

½ TEASPOON SALT

1 7/8 CUPS BROWN SUGAR,
PACKED DOWN

4 EGGS,
WELL BEATEN

1 TEASPOON VANILLA EXTRACT

1 CUP WALNUTS,
CHOPPED

Cover apricots with water, bring to a boil, then simmer for 10 minutes until tender. Drain and cool. Set aside.

Mix butter, sugar, and 2 cups of flour together until crumbly. Pack mixture into the bottom of a greased 9x13-inch pan. Bake in a 350°F. oven for 15 to 20 minutes until edges are light brown.

In a bowl, combine brown sugar and eggs. Add remaining flour, baking powder, salt, and vanilla. Stir in walnuts and apricots. Spread this mixture onto the partially baked crust, covering top completely. Bake 30 minutes until top is firm to touch. Cool in pan. Cut into pieces.

YIELD: 2 DOZEN PIECES

Granny Peter's Seed Loaf

4 CUPS ALL-PURPOSE FLOUR

4 TEASPOONS BAKING POWDER

1 TEASPOON SALT

5 TABLESPOONS BUTTER

¼ CUP SUGAR

½ TABLESPOON CARAWAY SEEDS

1 EGG

½ CUP MILK

Sift flour, baking powder, and salt together. Rub in the butter. Add the sugar and caraway seeds. Make a well in the center of the ingredients. Beat egg and milk together and pour into other ingredients. Mix to a soft dough. Put dough into a greased bread pan. Bake in a 350°F. oven for 1 hour, or until a skewer inserted in the crust comes out clean.

YIELD: 1 LARGE LOAF

Wholewheat Bread

1 CAKE COMPRESSED YEAST
OR 1 ENVELOPE DRY YEAST

2 TEASPOONS BROWN SUGAR

¾ CUP LUKEWARM WATER

1 TABLESPOON MOLASSES

¼ TEASPOON SALT

1 TABLESPOON LARD

12 CUPS WHOLEWHEAT FLOUR
(WARMED)

Dissolve yeast and brown sugar in ½ cup water. Dissolve molasses and salt in remaining warm water. Rub lard and flour together in a large bowl. Add the yeast and molasses mixtures. Mix to a firm dough until it comes away from the sides of the bowl. Add a little more tepid water if necessary, but do not make mixture too wet.

Knead dough for 5 minutes on a lightly floured board. Divide mixture in half and place into greased 10x4-inch warm pans. Cut two slits on top of each loaf.

Cover with clean cloths and let rise for about 1 hour, or until dough has doubled in size. Place in preheated 425°F. oven for 10 minutes, then reduce heat to 400°F. and continue baking for 30 to 35 minutes. Cool on wire rack.

YIELD: 2 LOAVES

Brown Bread

½ TEASPOON SUGAR

1 7/8 CUPS LUKEWARM WATER

1 CAKE COMPRESSED YEAST
OR 1 ENVELOPE DRY YEAST

3 CUPS (12 OUNCES) WHOLE BRAN
FLOUR

3 CUPS (12 OUNCES) ALL-PURPOSE
FLOUR

2 TEASPOONS SALT

2 TEASPOONS VEGETABLE OIL

Dissolve sugar in water and sprinkle in yeast.

Sift flours and salt together and return any bran left in sieve to the bowl. Add oil and yeast. Mix to a firm dough in a large greased loaf pan. Cover with greased plastic wrap and leave in a warm place to rise until doubled in size. Bake for 10 minutes at 475°F., for 35 minutes, or until brown. Cool on wire rack.

YIELD: 1 LARGE LOAF

Breakfast Rolls

1 CAKE COMPRESSED YEAST
OR 1 ENVELOPE DRY YEAST

½ TEASPOON SUGAR

5/8 CUP LUKEWARM WATER

5/8 CUP PLUS 2 TABLESPOONS MILK

¼ CUP BUTTER

4 CUPS ALL-PURPOSE FLOUR

½ TEASPOON SALT

Crumble yeast into small bowl. Mix in sugar and 2 tablespoons of water. Set in a warm place for 15 or 20 minutes.

In a small saucepan, scald 5/8 cup milk—do not boil. Remove pan from heat and add butter. Set pan aside and allow milk to cool to lukewarm.

Sift flour and salt into a large warmed bowl and make a well in the center. Add yeast and milk mixtures and remaining water. Gradually mix the flour and liquids together until all ingredients are incorporated and the dough comes away from the sides of the bowl. Knead dough on a lightly floured board for 10 minutes until smooth and elastic. Use more flour if board becomes sticky. Place the dough in a large, lightly greased bowl. Cover with a clean cloth, set in a warm place and allow dough to rise until doubled in bulk—about 1 to 1½ hours. Grease and flour a large baking sheet.

Turn the dough onto a lightly floured board and knead for 5 minutes. Divide the dough into 8 equal pieces and shape each piece into an oval. Place rolls on a large greased and floured baking sheet. Cover and let the dough rise again for 30 minutes. Brush each roll with the remaining 2 tablespoons of milk. Bake in a preheated 425°F. oven for 15 to 20 minutes, or until golden brown. Serve hot.

YIELD: 8 TO 10 ROLLS

Fruit Teabread

½ CUP BUTTER

1 CUP COLD TEA

1 CUP MIXED DRIED FRUIT
(RAISINS, CURRANTS, AND CANDIED
PEELS)

½ CUP BROWN SUGAR,
PACKED DOWN

2 CUPS PLUS 1 TABLESPOON ALL-
PURPOSE FLOUR

2 TEASPOONS BAKING POWDER

1 TEASPOON BAKING SODA

½ TEASPOON SALT

½ TEASPOON ALLSPICE

Put butter, tea, fruit, and brown sugar in a saucepan, bring to a boil and then reduce heat to a simmer for 4 minutes.

Sift flour and baking powder together. Mix dry ingredients into cooked ingredients. Mix well. Place mixture in a greased loaf pan and bake in a 350°F. oven for 1 to 1¼ hours. Loaf should sound hollow when tapped. Cool in pan.

YIELD: 1 LARGE LOAF

Bread Sticks

¼ CUP BUTTER

¾ TEASPOON SALT

1½ TABLESPOONS SUGAR

1 CUP MILK,
SCALDED

1 CAKE COMPRESSED YEAST
OR 1 ENVELOPE DRY YEAST

1 EGG WHITE,
LIGHTLY BEATEN

3½ CUPS ALL-PURPOSE FLOUR

Combine butter, salt, 1 tablespoon of sugar, and scalded milk. Let the mixture stand until it is lukewarm. Mix compressed yeast and remaining sugar together until liquified. Add yeast, sugar, and egg white to the cooled milk. If using dry yeast, reserve a little of the milk, combined with remaining sugar, to liquify.

Sift flour into milk mixture. Mix together until the dough leaves the side of the bowl. Knead dough on a lightly floured board for 10 minutes. Place dough in a bowl in a warm place to rise until doubled in size. Punch down dough and divide into 36 portions. Roll into sticks of pencil thickness. Place sticks on greased and floured baking sheets. Allow to rise for 30 minutes. Bake for 10 minutes in a preheated 425°F. oven, then reduce heat to 375°F. and bake for 12 to 15 minutes longer, or until crisp and brown. Cool on wire racks.

YIELD: 36 BREAD STICKS

Hot Cross Buns

A traditional Good Friday breakfast.

1½ CUPS MILK

¼ CUP BUTTER

1/3 CUP SUGAR PLUS 1 TEASPOON

½ CAKE COMPRESSED YEAST
OR 1 ENVELOPE DRY YEAST

1 EGG,
LIGHTLY BEATEN

2/3 CUP OF RAISINS AND CURRANTS,
MIXED

4 CUPS ALL-PURPOSE FLOUR

1/3 TEASPOON SALT

½ TEASPOON CINNAMON

½ TEASPOON ALLSPICE

1 TEASPOON SUGAR

1 EGG WHITE,
LIGHTLY BEATEN

SUGAR

3 TABLESPOONS CONFECTIONER'S
SUGAR

1 TABLESPOON FRESH LEMON JUICE

Scald milk, butter, and 1/3 cup sugar, then pour into large bowl. Cool to lukewarm.

Mix compressed yeast with 1 teaspoon sugar until liquified. If using dry yeast, reserve a little lukewarm milk to combine with the sugar to liquify. Combine yeast and milk. Add eggs, currants, and raisins.

Sift together flour, salt, cinnamon, and allspice. Add to milk mixture and mix until dough leaves the sides of the bowl. Turn dough onto a lightly floured board and knead for 5 minutes, or until dough is smooth. Place dough in a greased bowl, cover and let rise in a warm place for about 30 minutes, or until doubled in bulk.

Turn dough onto a lightly floured board and cut into 24 portions. Shape each portion into a round. Place the buns on a greased baking sheet and let rise for about 15 minutes. Mark a cross on each bun just before baking. Bake in preheated 350°F. oven for 15 to 20 minutes. Remove from oven and brush with egg white and sprinkle with sugar.

Return to oven for a minute or two to set glaze.

Mix confectioner's sugar and lemon juice. Decorate buns with the traditional cross.

YIELD: 24 BUNS

Chester Buns

Chester is the county seat or capital of the county of Cheshire, famous for its walled city and a great cathedral. Chester was the main shopping center for my family. At Christmas time we all boarded a local train for the 14-mile journey to shop and see panto-mime performances of "Mother Goose," "Dick Whittington," and "Red Riding Hood." Then we stopped at a teashop for Chester buns, served warm and buttered with pots of jam on the side.

4 CUPS ALL-PURPOSE FLOUR

2 TEASPOONS SALT

3 TABLESPOONS BUTTER

½ CAKE COMPRESSED YEAST OR ½ ENVELOPE DRY YEAST

1 TEASPOON SUGAR

2½ TABLESPOONS MILK, WARMED

1 EGG

5 OUNCES CONDENSED MILK

1 TABLESPOON SUGAR

1 TABLESPOON WARM WATER

Sift flour and salt into a large bowl. Rub in butter. Make a well in the middle. Mix compressed yeast with sugar until liquified. If using dry yeast, add a little of the warm milk to sugar and yeast to liquify. Add the warm milk and mix. Add egg and condensed milk to yeast mixture. Add to the flour. Mix to a smooth dough that leaves the sides of the bowl. Turn dough onto a lightly floured board. Knead for 5 minutes, or until smooth and elastic. Put dough into a greased bowl, cover, and let rise in a warm place until doubled in bulk. Punch dough down, then shape into 12 round buns. Place on a greased baking sheet and let rise again for 30 minutes. Bake in a preheated 425°F. oven for about 15 minutes until nicely browned. Combine sugar and water. Brush buns with glaze while still hot.

YIELD: 12 LARGE BUNS

Chelsea Buns or Sticky Buns

2 CUPS ALL-PURPOSE FLOUR

½ CAKE COMPRESSED YEAST
OR ½ ENVELOPE DRY YEAST

8 TABLESPOONS WARM MILK

½ TEASPOON SUGAR

½ TEASPOON SALT

2 TABLESPOONS BUTTER,
MELTED

1 EGG,
BEATEN

2 TABLESPOONS BROWN SUGAR

3 TABLESPOONS CURRANTS

1 TABLESPOON MIXED CANDIED PEEL,
CHOPPED

1 TABLESPOON HONEY

Sift 2 tablespoons of flour and blend with yeast, milk, and sugar. Let sit until frothy, about 25 to 30 minutes.

Sift together remaining flour and salt then add to yeast mixture. Mix in 1 tablespoon butter and egg, making a soft dough. Turn dough onto a lightly floured board and knead for 10 minutes, or until smooth and elastic. Put dough in greased bowl, cover, and set in warm place to rise until doubled in size, about 1 hour.

Punch dough down and knead for 2 or 3 minutes. Roll dough into a rectangle 9x12 inches. Brush top of dough with butter, Sprinkle with sugar, currants, and candied peel. Roll up the long side like a jelly roll. Pinch edges together to seal. Cut roll into 9 slices and place cut side down in a greased cake pan.

Cover with greased paper and let double in size, about 30 minutes. Bake buns in preheated 375°F. oven for 30 to 35 minutes. Remove from oven and brush tops with a brush dipped in honey.

YIELD: 9 BUNS

Bath Buns

4 CUPS ALL-PURPOSE FLOUR

1 TEASPOON SALT

1 CAKE COMPRESSED YEAST
OR 1 ENVELOPE DRY YEAST

½ CUP SUGAR

2 EGGS,
BEATEN

1/3 CUP BUTTER,
MELTED

1 CUP RAISINS

1 CUP MILK

3 TO 4 TABLESPOONS ALMONDS,
CHOPPED

SUGAR

Sift together flour and salt into a large bowl. Mix the compressed yeast with 1 teaspoon of sugar until liquified. If using dry yeast, use a little of the milk, lukewarm, combined with the sugar, to liquify. Make a hollow in the center of the flour. Add yeast, eggs, remaining sugar, butter, raisins, and milk. Mix until dough is stiff and leaves the sides of the bowl. Cover dough with a clean, damp cloth and allow to rise until double in bulk. Divide dough into 24 portions with a spoon or spatula. Handle as little as possible. Place the portions on greased baking sheets. Sprinkle each bun with almonds and sugar. Let buns rise for 30 minutes. Bake buns at 375°F. for 20 minutes or until tops are golden brown. Serve hot or cold.

YIELD: 24 BUNS

One-Egg Muffins

2 CUPS ALL-PURPOSE FLOUR

½ TEASPOON SALT

2 TEASPOONS BAKING POWDER

1 TABLESPOON LARD

1½ CUPS MILK

1 EGG,
WELL BEATEN

2 TABLESPOONS SUGAR

Sift together flour, salt, and baking powder into a large bowl. Rub in lard. Add sugar, egg, and milk. Beat very well. Fill greased muffin tins half full. Bake in 350°F. oven for 5 minutes. Raise oven temperature to 400°F. and bake muffins for 15 to 20 minutes until golden brown. Serve hot with butter and jam.

YIELD: 10 TO 12 MUFFINS

English Muffins

6 CUPS FLOUR

1 TEASPOON SALT

1½ PACKAGES DRY YEAST

2 TO 2½ CUPS MILK,
LUKEWARM

2 TABLESPOONS GROUND RICE

LARD FOR GRIDDLE

Sift flour and salt into a large bowl. Make a well in the center. Sprinkle yeast into ½ cup milk and let stand until dissolved. Pour yeast mixture into flour. Add 1½ cups of milk, adding just enough milk to make a soft dough. It should not be sticky. Turn dough onto a lightly floured board and knead for 5 minutes, or until smooth and elastic. Place dough in a warm greased bowl and cover with a damp cloth. Set in a warm place to rise until doubled in size, about 1 hour. Punch dough down and divide into 18 pieces. Sprinkle ground rice onto board. Pat dough into greased 4-inch muffin rings. Press both sides of dough in ground rice.

Transfer dough in the rings to a greased griddle or heavy skillet. Cook over low to moderate heat for 6 to 7 minutes until muffin rises and is lightly browned. Turn and cook other side. Remove muffin rings and cool. Split muffins and toast until golden brown. Serve with butter, jam, or honey.

Note: If muffin rings are not available, use 4-inch plain cookie cutters or shape rings from several thicknesses of aluminum foil.

YIELD: 18 MUFFINS

Cheese Scones

2 CUPS ALL-PURPOSE FLOUR

2 TEASPOONS BAKING POWDER

1 TABLESPOON BUTTER

2 OUNCES CHEDDAR CHEESE,
GRATED

PINCH OF SALT

2 TO 3 TABLESPOONS MILK

Sift flour and baking powder together. Rub in butter. Add cheese and salt. Add enough milk to make a light dough. On a lightly floured board roll dough into a large circle ½-inch thick. Cut circle into large or small triangles or into rounds. Place scones on an ungreased baking sheet and bake for 10 to 15 minutes in a 375°F. oven. Split scones in half and serve with lots of butter. The quantity depends on the size desired.

Oatcakes

A Scottish biscuit for cheese.

½ POUND MEDIUM OATMEAL,
CHOPPED

1 CUP ALL-PURPOSE FLOUR

½ TEASPOON SALT

3 TABLESPOONS BUTTER,
MELTED

2 TO 3 TABLESPOONS MILK

Combine oatmeal, flour, and salt. Mix butter into dry ingredients to make a stiff dough. Use a little warm milk if necessary to mix. Sprinkle a little oatmeal onto a wooden board.

Turn dough onto board and knead lightly. Work as fast as possible because dough drys quickly. Roll out to ¼-inch thickness. Cut into triangles or use a round cookie cutter. Place oatcakes on greased baking sheets and bake 8 to 10 minutes, or until golden brown in 375°F. oven. Cool on wire rack.

YIELD: 10 TRIANGLES OR
24 TWO-INCH CAKES

Notes

Sweet Dishes

The desserts I grew up with were from unsophisticated recipes—natural flavors with not too much added or too much taken away and always homemade from the best products to hand.

Blancmange is a familiar dessert in England. Made with cream and flavorings and usually served with a fruit jelly that is made with gelatin and fresh fruit juices, it is a welcome sweet at tea time, in or out of the nursery. Bread-and-butter pudding, rice pudding, trifle, junkets, creams, and syllabubs are some of the desserts I knew as a child and still adore. There are recipes that have survived for generations: cold weather puddings, tarts, flans, cakes for special occasions, even simple (but good) stewed fruit with cream.

Dessert has always been the highlight of a meal for me.

Blancmange

2 CUPS MILK

RIND OF 1 LEMON, THINLY PEELED

2 TABLESPOONS OF GELATIN

8 TABLESPOONS OF SUGAR

2 CUPS HEAVY CREAM

3 TABLESPOONS ALMONDS, GROUND

2 TABLESPOONS COGNAC

FRUIT JELLY (RECIPE FOLLOWS)

Soak lemon peel in milk for 1 hour. Strain.

Heat milk but do not boil. Dissolve gelatin in 2 tablespoons of milk. Add the gelatin to the remaining milk and stir in sugar. Blend in cream and almonds. Cook in a double boiler for 8 to 10 minutes, until mixture thickens. Let cool. Stir in cognac. Pour mixture into a mold that has been rinsed in cold water. Refrigerate to set. Unmold onto a serving dish. Surround blancmange with jelly.

NOTE: Omit cognac for children.

6 SERVINGS

Fruit Jelly

RIND OF 2 ORANGES,
THINLY SLICED

RIND OF 2 LEMONS,
THINLY SLICED

1 CUP SUGAR

2 WHOLE CLOVES

2 EGG WHITES,
LIGHTLY BEATEN

2½ CUPS WATER

½ CUP ORANGE JUICE

½ CUP LEMON JUICE

2 TABLESPOONS GELATIN

5 TABLESPOONS SHERRY
OR ADDITIONAL JUICE

Place orange and lemon rinds, sugar, cloves, egg whites, water, and juices in a pan. Bring slowly to a boil. Remove from heat and strain mixture through a double thickness of cheesecloth.

Dissolve gelatin in a little cold water and add to mixture. Simmer gently for 10 minutes. Remove from heat and stir in sherry. Cool for 30 minutes. Pour gelatin into a mold that has been rinsed in cold water. Refrigerate. To unmold, dip mold quickly into hot water and reverse on a plate. The fruit jelly also can be spooned around the blancmange.

Tea Cream

2 CUPS MILK

2 TABLESPOONS ORANGE PEKOE OR
SIMILAR TEA LEAVES

2 CUPS HEAVY CREAM,
LIGHTLY WHIPPED

2 TABLESPOONS GELATIN

8 TABLESPOONS SUGAR

Bring milk to a boil and pour over tea leaves. Cover and let tea infuse for 20 minutes. Strain, then fold in cream. Dissolve gelatin in a little boiling water and stir in. Add sugar and mix. Pour into a mold rinsed with cold water. Unmold and serve with freshly sliced peaches.

6 TO 8 SERVINGS

Treacle Jelly Cream

2 CUPS MILK

1 TABLESPOON GELATIN

1 TABLESPOON DARK MOLASSES

SWEET CHOCOLATE,
GRATED

WHIPPED CREAM

Put milk, gelatin, and molasses into a heavy saucepan. Heat until gelatin is dissolved. Stir constantly—do not boil. Pour into a mold rinsed under cold water. Refrigerate. Unmold and serve garnished with grated chocolate and a spoonful of whipped cream.

2 TO 3 SERVINGS

Prune Whip

Any pureed cooked fruit can be used.

2 TABLESPOONS CORNSTARCH

¾ CUP OF SUGAR

3 TABLESPOONS COLD WATER

1 CUP ORANGE JUICE

2 EGG WHITES

1 CUP COOKED PRUNES,
PITTED AND PUREED

JUICE AND GRATED RIND OF ½ LEMON

Combine cornstarch, sugar, and water. Bring orange juice to a boil. Stir boiling juice into cornstarch mixture. Return to heat and bring to a boil, stirring constantly so mixture does not get lumpy. Cook for 5 minutes. Remove from heat and cool for 10 minutes.

Beat egg whites until stiff. Fold into cornstarch mixture. Fold in prune puree, lemon rind, and juice. Spoon mixture into a bowl. Refrigerate. Serve with heavy cream.

4 SERVINGS

Floating Island

6 EGGS,
SEPARATED

4½ CUPS MILK

6 TABLESPOONS SUGAR

1 TEASPOON VANILLA

GRATED NUTMEG (OPTIONAL)

Beat egg whites until stiff. Bring 4 cups milk to a boil and add 3 tablespoons sugar. Drop tablespoonfuls of egg whites into boiling milk. Cook for a few seconds, then turn and cook briefly on the other side. Remove boiled whites with a slotted spoon and place in a flat dish. Continue until all whites are used up.

Beat egg yolks with remaining sugar until thick and lemon colored. Add ½ cup milk and mix well. Slowly add yolk mixture to hot milk. Cook mixture for one minute, stirring constantly. Add vanilla. Cool. Pour custard over the egg whites. Sprinkle with grated nutmeg. Chill before serving.

6 SERVINGS

Chocolate Mousse I

This is a special favorite dessert of my nephew, Keith. I always know what to make for dessert when he visits.

1 TABLESPOON GELATIN

¼ CUP COLD WATER

½ CUP BOILING WATER

2 OUNCES UNSWEETENED
CHOCOLATE

1 CUP SUGAR

1 TEASPOON VANILLA

2½ CUPS HEAVY CREAM

CHOCOLATE CURLS

Soak gelatin in cold water for 5 minutes. Melt chocolate in boiling water, then add gelatin. Stir well. Add sugar and vanilla. Cool.

Whip cream until stiff and fold into chocolate mixture. Spoon into glass bowl and refrigerate. Make chocolate curls from block chocolate that has been warmed gently. Use vegetable peeler to shave off long slivers of chocolate to decorate the mousse.

8 SERVINGS

Chocolate Mousse II

1 TABLESPOON GELATIN

3 TABLESPOONS COLD WATER

6 OUNCES SEMI-SWEET CHOCOLATE

½ CUP HOT MILK

3 EGGS,
SEPARATED

3 TABLESPOONS COGNAC

2 TABLESPOONS SUGAR

SALT

1 CUP HEAVY CREAM

Soften gelatin in cold water. Reserve. Melt chocolate in hot milk. Beat egg yolks slightly and add to melted chocolate. Stir over low heat until thickened. Mix in gelatin and cognac.

Beat egg whites with sugar and a pinch of salt until stiff. Fold into chocolate mixture. Whip cream until stiff. Fold into chocolate mixture. Spoon mousse into a serving bowl and refrigerate for 2 hours before serving.

8 SERVINGS

Lemon Mousse

4 EGGS,
SEPARATED

½ CUP SUGAR

1 TABLESPOON LEMON PEEL,
GRATED

1 TABLESPOON ORANGE PEEL,
GRATED

3 TABLESPOONS FRESH LEMON JUICE

1 CUP HEAVY CREAM

THIN LEMON SLICES

CANDIED VIOLETS (OPTIONAL)

Beat egg yolks with sugar until thick and lemon colored. Add grated peels and lemon juice, mixing well. Cook mixture in a double boiler over simmering water until thickened, stirring often. Let mixture cool.

Beat egg whites until stiff. Fold into egg mixture.

Beat heavy cream until stiff. Fold into mixture. Spoon mousse into a glass bowl. Chill.

Decorate mousse with lemon slices and candied violets.

4 TO 6 SERVINGS

Vanilla Mousse

3 EGGS,
SEPARATED

¾ CUP SUGAR

1 TABLESPOON VANILLA

¾ CUP MILK LESS 1 TABLESPOONFUL

1 ENVELOPE OF UNFLAVORED
GELATIN

2 CUPS HEAVY CREAM

GRATED CHOCOLATE

Beat egg yolks until light and lemon colored. Gradually add sugar and beat until thick and creamy. Add vanilla to ½ cup of milk. Mix into the egg yolks.

Soften gelatin in remaining milk and heat over low flame. Add milk-gelatin mixture to eggs. Blend thoroughly.

Beat egg whites until stiff and fold into mixture. Beat cream until stiff and blend into mixture. Pour into a serving bowl and chill for 2 hours before serving.

Sprinkle mousse with grated chocolate.

4 TO 6 SERVINGS

Lemon Cream

1 TABLESPOON UNFLAVORED
GELATIN

3 CUPS MILK

1 CUP SUGAR

PEEL OF 1 LEMON,
THINLY SLICED

3 EGGS

JUICE OF 2 LEMONS

1 PINT RASPBERRIES

Dissolve gelatin in milk. Add sugar and lemon peel. Bring mixture to a boil and cook gently for 5 minutes. Remove from heat and slowly add eggs to the hot milk, stirring constantly. Cool.

Blend in lemon juice when nearly cold. Strain mixture through a sieve into a mold. Chill for 2 hours before serving. Serve with fresh raspberries.

4 TO 6 SERVINGS

Baked Plums and Bread

8 LARGE RIPE PLUMS,
HALVED AND PITTED

4 TABLESPOONS BROWN SUGAR

4 SLICES WHITE BREAD,
TRIMMED AND BUTTERED

2 TABLESPOONS BUTTER

SUGAR

CINNAMON

FRESH CREAM

Fill each plum half with brown sugar. Arrange buttered bread slices in a shallow baking dish. Place plums on top of bread, cut side down. Dot plums with pieces of butter and sprinkle with brown sugar. Cover with buttered waxed paper and bake in a 375°F. oven until bread is browned, approximately 30 minutes. Remove dish from oven and sprinkle with sugar and cinnamon while still hot. Serve at once with heavy cream.

4 SERVINGS

English Rice Pudding

I make rice pudding in large amounts to serve hot and then eat leftovers the next day—cold, thick, creamy, and delicious.

2 TABLESPOONS BUTTER

7 TABLESPOONS RAW RICE

9 TABLESPOONS SUGAR

½ TEASPOON SALT

1 QUART MILK

1 8-OUNCE CAN EVAPORATED MILK

1 CUP WATER

1 TEASPOON LEMON PEEL,
GRATED

½ TEASPOON CINNAMON

¼ TEASPOON NUTMEG

Grease a large pudding dish with 1 tablespoon of butter. Place rice, sugar, and salt into dish. Add milk, evaporated milk, water, and lemon peel. Stir to mix well. Cut remaining butter into small pieces and float on top of the mixture. Sprinkle with nutmeg and cinnamon. Bake in a 300°F. oven for 2 hours.

NOTE: After pudding has been in the oven for about 1 hour, stir with a spoon. Try not to break the skin that forms on top. This becomes a pretty brown covering on the pudding. Let pudding stand for 30 minutes before serving.

8 TO 10 SERVINGS

Snowdon Pudding

A Welsh recipe.

4 OUNCES RAISINS

8 OUNCES BEEF SUET,
SHREDDED

8 OUNCES FRESH BREAD CRUMBS

1 CUP BROWN SUGAR,
LOOSELY PACKED

1½ OUNCES CORNSTARCH OR
GROUND RICE

¼ TEASPOON SALT

6 EGGS,
WELL BEATEN

6 OUNCES LEMON OR ORANGE
MARMALADE

GRATED PEEL OF 2 LEMONS

Reserve ¼ cup of raisins. Mix all dry ingredients and remaining raisins together. Mix in eggs, marmalade, and lemon peel. Place the ¼ cup of raisins in the bottom of a well-buttered bowl. Spoon the pudding mixture into the bowl. Cover top of bowl with a double thickness of wax paper. Secure paper with string. Place pudding in a pot and pour in enough boiling water to cover ¾ of the bowl. Cover pot and boil pudding for 1½ hours. Check water level from time to time and add boiling water if necessary.

Serve hot with Madeira or sherry sauce (recipe follows).

6 TO 8 SERVINGS

Madeira or Sherry Sauce

1½ TABLESPOONS SUGAR

PEEL OF ½ LEMON

4 TABLESPOONS WATER

1 TABLESPOON BUTTER

1 TEASPOON FLOUR

6 TABLESPOONS MADEIRA OR SHERRY

Boil sugar, lemon peel, and water for 10 to 15 minutes. Remove lemon peel.

Melt butter in a pan, then add flour, mixing well. Cook for a few minutes, remove from heat and add the water mixture. Stir vigorously to prevent lumps. Return to heat and bring back to a gentle boil. Remove from heat and add Madeira or sherry. Mix well. Serve hot over pudding.

Tipsy Trifle

AN 8-INCH SPONGE CAKE (PAGE 106)

¼ CUP SHERRY

½ CUP RASPBERRY JAM

2 CUPS CUSTARD SAUCE
(RECIPE FOLLOWS)

2 CUPS HEAVY CREAM,
WHIPPED

SLIVERED ALMONDS

Split sponge cake in half. Spread jam on cut sides and put back together. Place sponge cake in deep glass dish. Sprinkle cake with sherry. Cover cake with custard sauce. Cover custard with whipped cream. Sprinkle with almonds. Chill before serving.

6 SERVINGS

Custard Sauce

4 EGGS

6 TABLESPOONS SUGAR

2 CUPS MILK

1 ¼-INCH PIECE VANILLA BEAN OR
2 TEASPOONS VANILLA EXTRACT

Beat eggs with sugar until thick and lemon colored. Heat milk, then stir into eggs. Place mixture in top of double boiler, add vanilla bean and cook until custard is thick and creamy. Remove vanilla bean. If using vanilla extract, add after the sauce is cooked.

English Suet Pudding

Also called Spotted Dick.

3 CUPS ALL-PURPOSE FLOUR,
SIFTED

1 CUP RAISINS

1 TEASPOON BAKING SODA

1 TEASPOON CINNAMON

1 TEASPOON CLOVES

½ TEASPOON GRATED NUTMEG

1 TEASPOON SALT

1 CUP BEEF SUET,
SHREDDED

1 CUP SOUR MILK (ADD 1 TEASPOON
OF VINEGAR TO 1 CUP MILK)

1 CUP MOLASSES

Sift ½ cup flour over raisins and reserve.

Sift together the dry ingredients.
Combine suet, milk, and molasses.
Combine dry ingredients with milk-
molasses mixture. Mix well. Add the
floured raisins.

Butter 1 large or 2 small pudding
bowls and fill with mixture to ¾ full.
Cover with buttered wax paper.
Secure with string.

Fill pot with water and steam for 3
hours. Serve with custard sauce (page
144) or cream.

6 TO 8 SERVINGS

Custard Bread Pudding

2 CUPS (5 OR 6 SLICES) STALE
WHITE BREAD

1 QUART MILK

¼ TEASPOON SALT

2 EGGS

½ CUP SUGAR

1 TEASPOON VANILLA

½ CUP RAISINS (OPTIONAL)

Soak bread in milk until soft. Mash
the bread and milk together until fine.
Place bread and milk in a pan and heat
almost to boiling. Beat eggs until light,
then add sugar, salt, vanilla, and raisins.
Mix well. Stir this mixture into the
hot bread and milk. Pour into a 2-
quart baking dish. Set the dish in a
pan of water 2/3 of the way up the
sides of the dish. Bake in a 350°F.
oven for 45 minutes.

4 TO 6 SERVINGS

Cloutie Dumpling

This is a Scottish dish that resembles a Christmas pudding. Charms such as thimbles and silver sixpences are mixed into the pudding for special celebrations. A year of good fortune comes to those finding a charm.

3 CUPS ALL-PURPOSE FLOUR

1 CUP SUET,
FINELY SHREDDED

¾ CUP CURRANTS

¾ CUP LIGHT RAISINS

¾ CUP DARK RAISINS

3 TEASPOONS BAKING POWDER

½ TEASPOON BAKING SODA

½ TEASPOON CREAM OF TARTAR

¾ CUP BROWN SUGAR,
TIGHTLY PACKED

1½ TEASPOONS GROUND CINNAMON

1½ TEASPOONS GROUND GINGER

1½ TEASPOONS GROUND ALLSPICE

½ TART APPLE,
PEELED, CORED AND GRATED

1 EGG,
WELL BEATEN

4 TABLESPOONS MOLASSES

¾ CUP MILK

SUGAR

Combine flour, suet, currants, raisins, baking powder, baking soda, cream of tartar, brown sugar, and spices. Stir in apple. Make a well in the center of the ingredients. Mix egg and molasses together, then add to flour mixture. Add milk and stir until mixture is a soft dough.

Scald a dish towel with boiling water. Remove excess water from cloth and sprinkle one side with flour. Turn dumpling mixture onto the floured towel. Gather the sides of the cloth up to the top of the dumpling and tie loosely, allowing room for expansion.

Place in a large pot of boiling water, cover pot with a lid, and boil for 3 hours. Add boiling water to pot as necessary to keep dumpling covered. Drain, then set dumpling in a baking pan in a 350°F. oven for approximately 10 minutes to dry. Remove from oven and sprinkle with sugar. Serve hot with custard sauce (page 144), or brandy sauce (recipe follows). Any leftovers can be sliced and served fried in butter or with bacon for a breakfast treat the next day.

8 SERVINGS

Brandy Sauce

8 EGG YOLKS

6 TABLESPOONS SUGAR

1½ CUPS MILK

1 CUP HEAVY CREAM

4 TABLESPOONS BRANDY

Beat egg yolks and sugar together until light and creamy. Heat milk and cream but do not boil. Pour into eggs and sugar, mixing well. Strain. Place custard in double boiler and heat, stirring constantly until sauce thickens. Stir in brandy. Serve hot over cloutie dumpling or pour into a mold and refrigerate before serving cold.

Old-Fashioned Bread and Butter Pudding

8 SLICES WHITE BREAD,
TRIMMED AND BUTTERED

1 CUP RAISINS

GRATED PEEL OF 1 LEMON

4 TABLESPOONS BROWN SUGAR

1 CUP MILK

1 EGG,
WELL BEATEN

Butter a 3-cup baking dish. Cut each slice of bread into 3 portions. Arrange half of the pieces, buttered side down, in the baking dish. Cover with most of raisins, lemon peel, and 3 tablespoons of sugar. Cover with remaining bread, buttered side up. Sprinkle with remaining sugar, raisins, and lemon peel. Combine milk and egg together and strain over the pudding. Let pudding stand for 2 hours to soak up the liquid. Bake in a 350°F. oven for 40 to 45 minutes until puffed and browned. Serve hot or cold.

4 SERVINGS

Baked Princess Pudding

2 CUPS MILK

1 TABLESPOON BUTTER

GRATED PEEL AND JUICE OF 1 ORANGE

6 TABLESPOONS SUGAR

4 OUNCES FRESH BREAD CRUMBS

2 EGGS,
SEPARATED

3 TABLESPOONS APRICOT JAM

Slowly heat milk, butter, orange peel, and 3 tablespoons sugar. Remove from the heat and add bread crumbs. Mix and set aside for 15 minutes.

Beat egg yolks and mix into bread crumb mixture. Spoon mixture into a buttered 4-cup baking dish. Bake in a 325°F. oven for about 45 minutes until firm.

Combine apricot jam with orange juice. Spread over pudding.

Beat egg whites until stiff and fold in remaining sugar. Spoon meringue over pudding and return to oven for 15 to 20 minutes to lightly brown the topping. Serve hot.

4 TO 6 SERVINGS

Marmalade Pudding

½ CUP BUTTER

4 TABLESPOONS SUGAR

2 EGGS,
BEATEN

4 OUNCES BREAD CRUMBS

½ CUP FLOUR

1 TEASPOON BICARBONATE OF SODA

1 TABLESPOON MARMALADE

Cream butter and sugar. Add eggs and bread crumbs, mixing well. Sift together flour and bicarbonate. Add to mixture. Add marmalade and mix again. Butter a 3-cup pudding bowl and spoon mixture into the bowl. Cover with double thickness of wax paper. Secure with string. Put bowl into pot and add boiling water up to the lip of bowl. Put lid on pot and boil gently for 2 hours. Check water level from time to time and add more boiling water as necessary. Serve hot with custard sauce (page 144).

4 SERVINGS

Old English Plum Pudding

An expensive Christmas treat, but the best quality ingredients are a must. Plum pudding can be kept for 2 years, so you might as well make a big batch for gifts or to have on hand for special parties.

2 CUPS BRANDY

1 POUND CITRON PEEL,
FINELY CHOPPED

½ POUND CANDIED LEMON PEEL,
FINELY CHOPPED

½ POUND CANDIED ORANGE PEEL,
FINELY CHOPPED

½ POUND PITTED DATES,
FINELY CHOPPED

1 CUP BLANCHED ALMONDS,
FINELY CHOPPED

1 POUND CURRANTS

1 POUND RAISINS

1 POUND MUSCAT RAISINS

2 CUPS ALL-PURPOSE FLOUR

1 TEASPOON CINNAMON

¼ TEASPOON GROUND CLOVES

¼ TEASPOON GROUND GINGER

¼ TEASPOON GROUND NUTMEG

¼ TEASPOON GROUND MACE

1 POUND BEEF SUET,
GROUND

1 CUP DRIED BREAD CRUMBS

1 TEASPOON SALT

4 EGGS,
BEATEN

4 OUNCES CURRANT JELLY

2 TABLESPOONS BRANDY

Combine brandy and next 8 ingredients. Let stand for 24 hours, stirring once or twice.

Sift together flour and spices. Mix with suet, bread crumbs, and salt.

Add eggs and jelly to brandied fruits. Combine with flour mixture.

Pour into greased pudding bowls, leaving room for expansion. Cover each pudding with a double thickness of wax paper and secure with string around lip of bowl. Place each pudding bowl onto an 18-inch square, clean white cloth. Knot opposite corners on top of bowl, forming 2 knots. Place puddings in a large pot of boiling water. Boil large-sized pudding for 8 hours; if smaller, boil for 5 hours.

Lift pudding out of boiling water by the knots. Unwrap and unmold. Wrap puddings in several layers of cheesecloth moistened with brandy. Let pudding ripen in a cool place for 4 weeks, keeping the wrappings well soaked with brandy.

Unwrap puddings and steam for 3 hours to heat through. To serve, spoon 2 tablespoons brandy over the pudding, ignite, and bring to the table flaming. Serve with brandy or custard sauce (page 147 and 144) or heavy cream.

YIELD: 4 OR 5 TWO-POUND
PUDDINGS

Chester Pudding

1 CUP ALL-PURPOSE FLOUR

1 TEASPOON BAKING POWDER

4 OUNCES SHREDDED BEEF SUET

4 OUNCES BREAD CRUMBS

1 EGG,
BEATEN

4 TABLESPOONS BLACKCURRANT JAM

MILK

4 TABLESPOONS SUGAR

Sift flour and baking powder into a bowl. Add suet, bread crumbs, and sugar. Mix. Add egg, jam, and enough milk to make a soft dough. Put dough into a 4-cup pudding bowl. Cover with double thickness of wax paper and secure with string. Steam for **3** hours or place pudding bowl into a pot and add boiling water up to lip of pudding basin and boil gently for **3** hours. Check water level from time to time and add more boiling water if necessary. Serve hot with heavy cream.

4 TO 6 SERVINGS

Raisin-Peanut Bars

12 OUNCES BITTER-SWEET
CHOCOLATE

1 CUP DARK RAISINS

1 CUP PEANUTS,
CHOPPED

½ TEASPOON SALT

Melt chocolate in a double boiler and stir until smooth. Remove from heat and stir until nearly cool Add raisins, peanuts, and salt. Mix well. Spread to ¼-inch thick in a shallow pan. Store in a cool place until set and cut into pieces.

YIELD: 20 BARS

Rum Balls

3 POUNDS PLAIN CAKE OR COOKIE
PIECES (PREPARE VICTORIA SPONGE
CAKE ON PAGE 107 AND LET IT DRY
FOR 1 WEEK)

1 POUND SHELLED WALNUTS

1 POUND SEMI-SWEET CHOCOLATE

3 EGG WHITES,
LIGHTLY BEATEN

¼ CUP DARK RUM

1 TABLESPOON SUGAR

CONFECTIONER'S SUGAR

Grind cake, walnuts, and chocolate
through food chopper. Place in large
pan, add egg whites and mix. Sprinkle
rum over mixture. Mix and squeeze ingredients together with your hands.
Consistency should be quite stiff. If
more liquid is necessary, add rum.
Taste and add the sugar. Continue
working ingredients together. Roll into balls the size of walnuts, then roll
each rum ball in confectioner's sugar.
Place each rum ball in a paper bonbon
cup or on wax paper. Rum balls keep
several weeks in a cool temperature. If
the sugar coating disappears, reroll in
confectioner's sugar.

YIELDS: 75 TO 80 BALLS

Apricot Balls

4 OUNCES DRIED APRICOTS,
FINELY CHOPPED

3 OUNCES CREAM CHEESE

2 OUNCES STALE PLAIN CAKE CRUMBS

2 OUNCES CONFECTIONER'S SUGAR

4 OUNCES PLAIN CHOCOLATE

ALMOND EXTRACT

Combine apricots and add cream
cheese until smooth. Add cake crumbs
and sugar, mixing well. Flavor to taste
with almond extract. Roll mixture
into small balls the size of marbles. If
mixture becomes sticky, roll in some
confectioner's sugar.

Melt chocolate over hot water. Spear
the apricot balls with a skewer and dip
each ball into the melted chocolate,
coating thoroughly. Place on lightly
greased wax paper. Chill.

YIELD: 20 TO 24 BALLS

Truffles

2 OUNCES CHOCOLATE,
GRATED

1 OUNCE CONFECTIONER'S SUGAR

1 TEASPOON IRISH MIST OR RUM

HEAVY CREAM

1 TABLESPOON PISTACHIO NUTS,
CHOPPED

2 TABLESPOONS CHOCOLATE
SPRINKLES

Mix chocolate and sugar. Stir in liquor and add enough heavy cream to make a stiff paste. Make small balls. Mix chocolate sprinkles and nuts together, then roll chocolate balls in mixture.

YIELD: 12 TRUFFLES

Rum Truffles

4 OUNCES MARZIPAN (PAGE 192)

1 TABLESPOON RUM

CHOCOLATE SPRINKLES

Flatten marzipan with the hand, making a little well in the center. Pour rum into the well and knead. Break off small pieces and form into balls. Roll balls in the chocolate sprinkles.

YIELD: 12 TO 15 TRUFFLES

Ginger Fudge

½ CUP EVAPORATED MILK

½ CUP MILK

2 CUPS GRANULATED SUGAR

4 TABLESPOONS SWEET BUTTER

2 TEASPOONS GROUND GINGER

2 TEASPOONS WATER

Place evaporated milk, milk, sugar, and butter in a heavy saucepan. Heat gently, stirring constantly, until mixture reaches soft ball stage, about 236°F. on a candy thermometer. Remove pan from heat. Combine ginger and water then stir into mixture, beating thoroughly with wooden spoon until it becomes thick and slightly coarse in texture. Pour immediately into a 6x4x1-inch deep greased pan. Cool and mark into pieces with a knife. Cut when fudge is firm.

YIELD: 16 PIECES

Chocolate Fudge

2 CUPS SUGAR

2 OUNCES OF BAKER'S CHOCOLATE, GRATED

1/8 TEASPOON CREAM OF TARTAR

2/3 CUPS MILK

1 TEASPOON VANILLA

1 TABLESPOON BUTTER

Combine sugar, milk, chocolate, and cream of tartar in heavy saucepan. Slowly bring to a boil, stirring constantly. Bring mixture to soft ball stage, about 236°F. on a candy thermometer. Remove from heat and add butter, but do not stir in. When mixture is lukewarm, add vanilla and beat until mixture thickens and the fudge holds its shape. Spread mixture in a 6x4x1-inch deep greased pan. Mark into squares and cut when firm.

YIELD: 16 PIECES

Sweet Pancakes

In England pancakes are traditionally served on Shrove Tuesday with a sprinkling of sugar and a squeeze of fresh lemon juice. I also enjoy the Hungarian pancakes (Turos palascinta) that Mama made, served with a pot cheese filling. The batter is the same and you can choose the filling.

2 CUPS ALL-PURPOSE FLOUR,
SIFTED

1 TEASPOON SALT

2 TEASPOONS SUGAR

4 EGGS,
WELL BEATEN

2 CUPS MILK

BUTTER

Mix flour, salt, and sugar. Combine eggs and milk. Gradually add liquid to flour, beating to a smooth, thin batter. Melt a small amount of butter in skillet. When skillet is hot, pour ¼ cup of batter into the skillet, and gently tip skillet from side to side to cover bottom of pan. Lightly brown pancake on both sides. Continue until all the batter is used up. Stack pancakes on a warm plate.

If using sugar and lemon juice, sprinkle each pancake, then roll up and keep warm until served.

If using pot cheese filling, spread filling (recipe follows) on each pancake, roll up, and place in buttered baking dish. Sprinkle with confectioner's sugar and heat for about 25 minutes in a 300°F. oven. Serve topped with sour cream and strawberry preserves.
YIELD: 20 PANCAKES

Cheese Filling

1 POUND POT CHEESE

1 EGG,
WELL BEATEN

½ CUP SUGAR

½ TEASPOON VANILLA

Mix all ingredients together.

Hungarian Doughnuts (Fánk)

These are heavier than the usual doughnut. They are best eaten hot, but can be reheated, wrapped in foil, in a 350°F. oven for 10 minutes. Mama always made huge panfuls of Fánk for her family during harvest time.

1 CAKE FRESH YEAST OR
1 OUNCE DRY YEAST

1 TABLESPOON SUGAR

3 CUPS MILK,
LUKEWARM

4 EGG YOLKS,
BEATEN

2 TABLESPOONS BUTTER,
MELTED

6 CUPS FLOUR

1 TEASPOON SALT

½ CUP LIGHT RAISINS

LARD

CONFECTIONER'S SUGAR

In a large bowl, combine yeast, sugar and milk. Set aside. Mix yolks and butter together, then combine with the yeast mixture. Mix flour, yeast mixture, salt, and raisins. Add to liquid mixture and mix to a soft dough with a wooden spoon, beating thoroughly. Let dough stand for 1 hour. Roll out dough on a lightly floured board to about 1-inch thickness. Cut out with doughnut cutter and let stand on floured board for 1 hour.

Fry in deep fat until golden brown. Remove from fat with slotted spoon and drain on paper towels. Dust generously with confectioner's sugar.

YIELD: 48 TO 60

Crumpets

4 CUPS ALL-PURPOSE FLOUR

½ TEASPOON BICARBONATE OF SODA

3 OUNCES BROWN SUGAR

1 EGG,
WELL BEATEN

2 CUPS MILK

Sift flour and soda together. Add sugar. Mix egg with milk. Gradually add liquid to flour and mix to a smooth batter. Cook like pancakes in a greased electric fry skillet heated to 350°F. Crumpet rings are used at Country Host but aluminum foil circles are satisfactory for controlling the size. Brown crumpets on both sides—little holes appear in the batter as it cooks. Keep hot and serve with lots of butter, honey, jam, or golden molasses.

4 TO 6 SERVINGS

Pikelets or Crumpets

Another form of crumpet.

6 CUPS FLOUR,
WARMED

1 TEASPOON SALT

½ OUNCE DRY YEAST

4 TO 4½ CUPS MILK,
LUKEWARM

Use 4-inch crumpet rings.

Sift flour and salt into a bowl. Make a well in the center.

Sprinkle yeast into ½ cup lukewarm milk and let stand until dissolved, about 5 minutes. Pour yeast mixture into the well in the flour. Add 3½ cups milk. Add the other ½ cup if necessary to make a consistency similar to pancake batter. Beat mixture for 5 minutes or until smooth and elastic with your hands or a large wooden spoon. Cover with a damp cloth and let rise until bubbles show through surface of batter, about 45 minutes. Punch batter down lightly.

Grease 3 or 4 crumpet rings. Set the rings on a hot greased griddle. Pour ½-inch batter into each ring. Cook over moderate heat until browned, about 7 or 8 minutes. Remove crumpet rings, turn the pikelet and cook the other side 3 or 4 minutes until gently browned. Do not brown too much. Serve for tea with butter, honey, jam, or molasses.

YIELD: 20 TO 24

Drop Scones or Scotch Pancakes

2 CUPS ALL-PURPOSE FLOUR

1 TEASPOON CREAM OF TARTAR

½ TEASPOON BICARBONATE OF SODA

1 TABLESPOON SUGAR

1 EGG

½ CUP MILK

BUTTER

Sift together flour, cream of tartar, bicarbonate of soda, and sugar. Beat egg with milk. Add to dry ingredients to form a batter. Mix well.

Lightly grease a heavy skillet or griddle with butter. When skillet is medium hot, add 2 teaspoons of mixture for each pancake. Cook on one side until golden brown, then turn and cook other side until golden. Serve hot with butter and jam.

YIELD: 20 SMALL PANCAKES

Banana Fritters

FRITTER BATTER (PAGE 190)

6 BANANAS, PEELED

2 TABLESPOONS SUGAR

3 OR 4 TABLESPOONS ORANGE JUICE

VEGETABLE OIL

Prepare the batter. Cut each banana in two and split in half. Put the pieces into a deep bowl with mixture of sugar and orange juice. Let stand for 1 hour.

Drain on paper towels. Dip each piece into batter. Fry in hot vegetable oil. Remove from fat with slotted spoon and drain. Serve hot.

6 SERVINGS

Apple Fritters

Pineapple pieces, oranges, apricots, or raspberries make delicious fruit fritters too.

6 TART APPLES,
PEELED, CORED AND SLICED INTO
¼-INCH RINGS

FRITTER BATTER (PAGE 190)

VEGETABLE OIL

CONFECTIONER'S SUGAR

Prepare batter using 2 eggs. Separate egg and add yolks to flour. Beat egg whites until stiff but not dry, then fold into mixture.

Coat apple rings, fry in hot vegetable oil, and drain. Sprinkle with confectioner's sugar before serving.

6 SERVINGS

Fresh Fruit Cup

3 BANANAS,
SLICED

JUICE OF 1 LEMON

½ PINEAPPLE,
PEELED AND DICED

1 CUP STRAWBERRIES,
SLICED

2 ORANGES,
CHOPPED

3 PEARS,
PEELED, CORED, AND CHOPPED

3 APPLES,
PEELED, CORED, AND CHOPPED

SMALL BUNCH BLACK GRAPES,
SEEDED AND SLICED

SMALL BUNCH GREEN GRAPES,
SEEDED AND SLICED

1 SMALL CANTALOUPE,
PEELED AND DICED

SUGAR

Coat the bananas with lemon juice. Mix all fruits together, including lemon juice from bananas. Chill. Some sugar may be added to taste.

8 SERVINGS

Stuffed Peaches

6 LARGE PEACHES,
PEELED

RAISINS, APPLES, OR GRAPES

SUGAR

NUTMEG

Cut a slice from each peach and remove pits without breaking the fruit. Fill the hollow with any chopped fruit such as raisins, apples, or green and black grapes. Sprinkle with a little sugar and a pinch of nutmeg. Bake in a 350°F. oven for 20 minutes, until sugar is melted into chopped fruit. Serve with cold soft custard (recipe follows).

6 SERVINGS

Soft Custard

2 CUPS MILK

2 WHOLE EGGS OR 4 EGG YOLKS

4 TABLESPOONS SUGAR

1/8 TEASPOON SALT

½ TEASPOON VANILLA OR 2-INCH
PIECE OF VANILLA BEAN

Scald milk in a double boiler. Lightly beat together eggs, sugar, and salt. Add hot milk to the egg mixture, beat well with a whisk, and return to the top of the double boiler. Cook over hot water, stirring constantly until mixture thickens. Add vanilla and mix. Let custard cool, then chill until ready to serve. To keep skin from forming on custard, cover dish with a plate or aluminum foil.

NOTE: If using vanilla bean, add it to the milk while scalding, then remove.

6 SERVINGS

Baked Pears

6 LARGE PEARS,
PEELED AND CORED

6 TABLESPOONS SUGAR

GRATED RIND OF 1 LEMON

1 TABLESPOON CANDIED GINGER,
CHOPPED

3 EGG WHITES

¼ CUP POWDERED SUGAR

WATER

Place pears in a baking dish. Combine sugar, lemon rind, and ginger. Fill the centers with the mixture. Add 3 or 4 tablespoons water to dish and bake for approximately 40 minutes in a 350°F. oven until pears are tender. Remove from oven.

Beat egg whites and sugar until stiff. Cover pears with meringue and brown quickly under the broiler. Serve at room temperature.

6 SERVINGS

Baked Rhubarb

6 CUPS RHUBARB,
CUT INTO 1-INCH PIECES

1½ CUPS SUGAR

PINCH OF SALT

PEEL OF 1 LEMON

Combine the ingredients. Place in a large covered dish and bake in a 375°F. oven for 25 to 30 minutes, or until rhubarb is tender. Cool and serve with fresh cream.

4 TO 6 SERVINGS

Raspberries

One can make raspberry turnovers (triangles of puff pastry filled with raspberries), raspberry jam, or raspberry short cake but I think bowls of fresh raspberries topped with vanilla ice cream or whipped cream is the best dessert ever. We had raspberries last year that were as big as thimbles. A huge basket of raspberries was poured over a gallon of vanilla ice cream, the ice cream was allowed to soften, then guests were served dishes of this fantastic combination. I now find it hard on my psyche to cook or crush raspberries—I just serve them whole and fresh.

Strawberries

Strawberries with clotted cream is a favorite dessert in England. Clotted cream is not readily available in America, but if one wishes to go to the trouble, it can be made.

Bring one quart plain pasturized milk almost to the boiling point. Pour into a shallow dish and leave out overnight to cool. The cream rises to the top of the dish, thick and light yellow in color. The clotted cream is skimmed off and chilled. Whipped cream can be substituted with much less trouble and fuss.

Strawberries and fresh pineapple pieces make a favorite dessert tray for many menus I prepare. A dish of confectioner's sugar is included on the tray. A rich dessert is not necessary, especially following a heavy meal.

Apples

I've always felt that apples are un-equaled in taste and unrivaled in beauty, and their blossoms are so fragrant. When our old orchard is in bloom, I feel renewed. In late May the branches are laden with pink and white blossoms. Gradually they turn into little green apples and these grow and change into rosy fruit. In October we get our windfall apples from the trees, and that's when I make apple-butter—dark brown and delicious.

When the wind and ice in winter tear down a limb or two of an old apple tree, we rescue the wood, dry it and use it for our winter fires. Burning apple wood has a marvelous smell.

Most of our trees are huge and they should be severely pruned, but the branches form such lovely patterns that I leave them alone. We have planted new trees to replace the producing part of the orchard. The old orchard will remain untouched for its beauty.

Apple Charlotte

2 POUNDS TART APPLES,
PEELED, CORED, AND SLICED

½ TEASPOON GROUND CINNAMON

1 CUP SUGAR

RIND AND JUICE OF ½ LEMON

¼ CUP WATER

8 OR 9 SLICES OF WHITE BREAD,
TRIMMED

½ CUP BUTTER,
MELTED

3 OR 4 PLAIN BUTTER COOKIES MADE
INTO CRUMBS (A SLICE OF STALE
CAKE CAN ALSO BE USED)

Cook apples with cinnamon, sugar, and lemon rind in water until soft. Trim bread slices to fit an 8-inch cake pan. Butter the pan, dip the bread slices in-to melted butter, and line the sides and bottom of the pan. Add bread crumbs and lemon juice to the apples. Spoon this mixture into the tin. Top with strips of buttered bread and sprinkle with sugar. Bake in a 375°F. oven for 1 hour. Cool, remove from pan, and serve with heavy cream.

6 SERVINGS

Pippins and Port

This dessert is usually served cold at Christmas. Allow time for the apples to soak overnight. The English recipe calls for Orange Pippins but Granny Smiths will do.

1 CUP SUGAR

2 CUPS WATER

1-INCH CINNAMON STICK

1 OUNCE FRESH GINGER

RIND OF 1 LEMON

1 CUP PORT

2 POUNDS APPLES,
PEELED AND CORED

Boil sugar, water, cinnamon, ginger, and lemon rind for 10 minutes. Strain into a dish and cool. Pour syrup over the apples and let them soak overnight.

Next day, transfer apples and syrup to a saucepan and simmer over a low flame until tender. Place apples in a serving dish. Add port to the hot syrup, strain, and pour over the apples. Serve chilled with whipped cream.

6 TO 8 SERVINGS

Baked Apples

As children we ate baked apples and custard at least once a week.

6 APPLES,
CORED

12 TEASPOONS BROWN SUGAR

6 TABLESPOONS BUTTER

½ CUP WATER

Fill the cavity of each apple with 2 teaspoons brown sugar and dot with 1 tablespoon butter. Place the apples in a shallow baking dish, add ½ cup water, and bake in a 350°F. oven for 45 to 50 minutes, or until the skins are cracked. Remove from the oven and baste with the juices. Cool and serve with soft custard (page 159) or whipped cream. For a variation, soak 6 tablespoons of raisins in 6 tablespoons sherry, mix with brown sugar and proceed as before.

6 SERVINGS

Potted Apples

This is a simple variation of stewed apples.

1 OUNCE FRESH GINGER

½ CUP WHISKY

8 MEDIUM APPLES,
PEELED, CORED, AND SLICED

3 CUPS SUGAR

JUICE OF 2 LARGE LEMONS

1 CUP WATER

Crush ginger and put in a jar with whisky. Cover and let stand for 3 days. Strain the whisky.

Put apples, sugar, lemon juice, whisky, and water into a pan. Cook gently until the apples are soft and transparent, being careful not to break slices. Cool and serve with whipped cream.

6 SERVINGS

Apple Dumplings

8 TABLESPOONS BUTTER

1 CUP BROWN SUGAR

¼ TEASPOON CINNAMON

GRATED RIND OF 2 LEMONS

8 LARGE COOKING APPLES,
PEELED AND CORED

DOUBLE RECIPE SWEET SHORTCRUST
PASTRY (PAGE 195)

1 EGG,
BEATEN WITH 2 TABLESPOONS WATER

SUGAR

Mix butter, sugar, cinnamon, and lemon rind together. Press this mixture into the apples.

Roll out the pastry and cut into 8 rounds, large enough to wrap around each apple. Moisten edges with egg and seal. Put the apples, sealed edges down, on a baking sheet. Brush with egg and sprinkle with sugar. Bake in a 350°F. oven for 1 hour, or until the apples are soft when tested with a fork and the pastry is golden brown. Serve warm with whipped cream.

8 SERVINGS

Apple and Rice Pudding

2 CUPS MILK

2 TABLESPOONS LONG-GRAIN RICE

4 TABLESPOONS SUGAR

1 CUP HEAVY CREAM

4 TABLESPOONS APRICOT JAM

2 CUPS STEWED APPLES

3 TABLESPOONS ALMONDS,
GROUND

1 EGG

Bring milk to a boil. Stir in rice and cook gently for about 40 minutes. Sweeten with 2 tablespoons sugar. Cool slightly.

Whip cream until thick but not stiff. Fold cream into the rice. Spread a layer of jam on the bottom of a deep pie dish, then a layer of stewed apples and then a layer of rice. Repeat until the dish is 2/3 full. Mix almonds with remaining sugar and egg. Spoon this mixture over the pudding. Bake in a 350°F. oven for 35 minutes. Serve hot with jam sauce (recipe follows) or heavy cream.

4 SERVINGS

Jam Sauce

1 CUP APRICOT JAM,
SIEVED

½ CUP WATER

1 TABLESPOON CORNSTARCH

JUICE OF 1 LEMON

Simmer jam and water for 5 minutes. Blend cornstarch with a little cold water, and stir a bit of the hot jam mixture into it. Pour this back into the jam mixture. Bring to a boil and stir until sauce is thick and clear. Add lemon juice and serve immediately.

Steamed Apple Suet Pudding

Suet is the fat from around a beef kidney—your butcher will be able to provide it.

1 POUND ALL-PURPOSE FLOUR

2 TEASPOONS BAKING POWDER

1 TEASPOON SALT

4 TO 5 MEDIUM APPLES,
PEELED, CORED, AND DICED

½ POUND SUET,
CHOPPED

4 OUNCES SUGAR

WATER

Sift together flour, baking powder, and salt. Add suet, apples, and sugar. Add just enough cold water to make a soft dough. Put mixture into a 2½-pint pudding basin. Steam for 2½ hours. Serve with hot soft custard (page 159). If you don't have a steam pot, cover pudding with buttered wax paper. Secure the paper with strings. Place the pudding basin in a pan of hot water filled almost to the top of the basin. Place in a 350°F. oven for 2½ hours. Add more hot water to pan if necessary.

4 SERVINGS

Quince Cream

Quinces are not easily found today. They look like big yellow apples and have a wonderful fragrance. Usually I find only 6 or 8—not enough to preserve, but plenty to make a delicious dessert for the family.

6 TO 8 MEDIUM QUINCE

6 TABLESPOONS SUGAR

1 TEASPOON GROUND GINGER

1 CUP HEAVY CREAM

Wipe quince with a damp cloth. Bake whole in a 400°F. oven for 45 minutes or until soft. Cool. Scrape out and mash the pulp. Combine pulp, sugar, ginger, and cream. Spoon into dessert dishes and serve warm or cold.

4 TO 6 SERVINGS

Notes

Jams, Preserves, and Pickles

Before preparing a recipe, sterilize the jars. I use 8-ounce jelly jars with screw tops, but any size will do if it can be completely sealed. Wash jars in soapy water, rinse well, and turn upside down on a baking sheet. Place in a 300°F. oven for 30 minutes. Fill jars while hot.

Strawberry Jam

The smell of strawberries cooking is unequaled. I am always anxious for them to ripen so I can get cracking with jam making.

7 POUNDS STRAWBERRIES,
STEMMED AND CRUSHED

12 CUPS SUGAR

JUICE OF 4 LEMONS

Put strawberries into a large pot and bring to a boil. Remove from heat. Add sugar and lemon juice and return to a boil, constantly stirring. If the jam starts to rise, lower the heat. Skim off the foam—it detracts from the looks of the jam. After 15 minutes of fast cooking, test the jam by placing a tablespoonful on a clean saucer and letting it cool. Tip the saucer—if it puckers, it is done. If not, keep boiling the jam and test again. It takes about 20 to 25 minutes.

When the jam puckers, remove pot from the stove. Working as quickly as possible, ladle the hot jam into the sterilized jars. Screw the tops on tightly.

YIELD: 17 TO 18
EIGHT-OUNCE JARS

Peach Preserves

I usually triple this recipe, but this is enough to start with.

3 CUPS SUGAR

2 CUPS WATER

2 POUNDS PEACHES,
PEELED AND PITTED

Boil sugar and water together until syrup coats the spoon. Add peaches and boil until syrup is thick. Place peaches in hot jars. Fill jars with hot syrup. Seal.

YIELD: 3 HALF-PINT JARS

Pear Marmalade

This is wonderful on hot scones.

8 POUNDS RIPE PEARS,
CORED

3 ORANGES,
SEEDED

2 LEMONS,
SEEDED

12 CUPS SUGAR

Grind whole pieces of fruit, including skin, in a food mill. Place fruit in a large pot, add sugar and stir well. Bring to a boil and cook until clear. Pour into hot glasses. Seal.

YIELD: 8 PINTS

Cherry and Raspberry Jam

2 CUPS CHERRIES,
PITTED

2 CUPS RASPBERRIES

4 CUPS SUGAR

Crush cherries lightly and cook until skins are tender. Add raspberries and simmer until mixture begins to thicken. Add sugar and cook rapidly until thick. Remove from heat and cool slightly. Pour into hot jars and seal.

YIELD: 7 EIGHT-OUNCE JARS

Plum Jam

Stirring the jam keeps the fruit from floating to the top of the jar. I suggest making this small amount first.

1 POUND PLUMS

1 CUP WATER

1½ CUPS SUGAR

Cook plums in boiling water until skins are tender, about 10 to 15 minutes. Cool and remove pits. Add sugar. Heat slowly until sugar is dissolved, then cook rapidly until thick. Cool a little and stir occasionally. Pour into hot jars and seal.

YIELD: 2 EIGHT-OUNCE JARS

Dundee Marmalade

1 POUND SEVILLE ORANGES

1 LEMON

2 PINTS WATER

4 CUPS SUGAR,
(WARMED OVER A PAN OF
HOT WATER)

Place whole oranges and lemon in a large heavy pot. Add water, cover and then simmer for 1½ hours, or until skins are soft and easily pierced. Remove the fruit and cool. Cut fruit into thin slices. Put pips from fruit back into the juice. Boil juice for 10 minutes, then skim out pips. Add oranges and lemon to the juice. Bring to a boil, then stir in sugar. When sugar dissolves, stir until mixture boils. Cook rapidly without stirring for about 20 minutes until mixture reaches setting stage. The marmalade is done when a teaspoonful placed on a saucer wrinkles when the saucer is tilted. Ladle marmalade into sterilized hot jars. Store in a cool place.

YIELD: 7 EIGHT-OUNCE JARS

Apple Butter

Apple butter takes at least 4 hours to cook, but it is well worth the effort.

Peel, core and slice 15 pounds of apples. Cortlands are an excellent choice. Place apples in a heavy pot with 1 quart natural cider. Bring to a boil, stirring often. Reduce heat and simmer for 2 hours. Remove from heat and crush apple pieces with a potato masher. Add 1 cup brown sugar if you like a sweeter butter. Return to the heat and continue simmering for another 2 hours. The mixture should be dark brown and thick. Spoon into hot, sterilized jars. Store in a cool place.

YIELD: 8 QUARTS

Carrot, Apple, and Peach Marmalade

1 PINT CARROTS,
DICED

1 PINT TART APPLES,
DICED

1 CUP PEACHES,
DICED

JUICE OF 1 LEMON

3 CUPS SUGAR

Combine all the ingredients and boil rapidly until mixture is clear. Pour into hot jars and seal.

YIELD: 2½ PINTS

Rhubarb Jam

My favorite.

2½ POUNDS RHUBARB,
CUT INTO 1-INCH PIECES

3 CUPS SUGAR

½ CUP WATER

RIND AND JUICE OF 2 ORANGES

Combine rhubarb, sugar, and water in a large pot. Add orange rind, and juice. Cook over medium heat for about 30 minutes, stirring often. Fill hot jars and seal.

YIELD: 9 EIGHT-OUNCE JARS

Apple Jelly

Green-skinned apples give the best color and tart apples have the highest natural pectin content.

6 POUNDS APPLES,
CORED AND QUARTERED

1 CUP WATER

SUGAR

JUICE OF 1 LEMON

Place apples and water in a heavy pot. Cook until apples are a soft pulp. Strain pulp through a sterilized muslin cloth or jelly bag. Do not squeeze or press the fruit—it clouds the jelly. The best method is to let the fruit drip overnight through the muslin.

Measure the juice. For each pint of juice, use 1 pound sugar. Place juice and sugar into a large heavy pot. Add lemon juice and stir over low heat until sugar is dissolved. Bring to a rapid boil, stirring frequently. After 10 minutes, test for setting. If necessary, boil mixture for another 5 minutes until testing shows the jelly is set.

Pour into sterilized screw-top jars. Store in a cool place.

YIELD: 8 OR 9 EIGHT-OUNCE JARS

Apple Chutney I

3 RED PEPPERS,
HALVED AND SEEDED

3 GREEN PEPPERS,
HALVED AND SEEDED

12 TART APPLES,
PEELED AND CORED

12 MEDIUM-RIPE TOMATOES

6 MEDIUM ONIONS

2 OUNCES CRYSTALLIZED GINGER

1 POUND SEEDLESS RAISINS

1 CUP CELERY,
DICED

2 QUARTS CIDER VINEGAR

3 CUPS SUGAR

2 TABLESPOONS SALT

Put peppers, apples, tomatoes, onions, ginger, raisins, and celery through a food mill. Combine all the ingredients and cook about 1 hour until thick and clear. Fill hot sterilized jars and seal.

YIELD: 8 PINTS

Apple Chutney II

A great favorite as an accompaniment for pork.

3 POUNDS TART APPLES,
PEELED, CORED AND SLICED

3 POUNDS ONIONS,
PEELED AND CHOPPED

1 POUND RAISINS

JUICE AND RIND OF 2 LEMONS

1½ POUND BROWN SUGAR

2 CUPS MALT VINEGAR

Put apples, onions, and raisins into a heavy pot. Add lemon juice and rind, sugar, and vinegar. Bring to a boil, stirring often. Reduce heat and simmer until mixture is thick and no liquid remains. Put into 7 or 8 hot, sterilized jars. Cool, then store.

YIELD: 7 OR 8 EIGHT-OUNCE JARS

Peach Chutney

¼ POUND CELERY,
CHOPPED

1 POUND PEACHES,
PEELED, PITTED, AND CHOPPED

½ POUND TART APPLES,
PEELED, CORED, AND CHOPPED

1 SWEET RED PEPPER,
CHOPPED

1½ CUPS CIDER VINEGAR

2 CUPS SUGAR

1 TEASPOON SALT

1 CUP SEEDLESS RAISINS

Cook celery in small amount of water until almost tender, then drain. Combine all ingredients except raisins and boil rapidly until clear and slightly thick.

Steam the raisins for 20 minutes in a colander over a pot of boiling water. Add to cooked ingredients. Pour into hot jars and seal.

YIELD: 2 PINTS

Mustard Pickle

1 SMALL CAULIFLOWER,
CUT INTO SMALL SPRIGS

1 MEDIUM CUCUMBER,
UNPEELED AND CUBED

3 MEDIUM ZUCCHINI OR SQUASH,
PEELED AND CUBED

4 TABLESPOONS SHALLOTS
OR ONIONS,
PEELED AND MINCED

1 TABLESPOON SALT

2 CUPS MALT VINEGAR

2 TEASPOONS DRY MUSTARD

1 TEASPOON DRY GINGER

1 TEASPOON TURMERIC

½ CUP ALL-PURPOSE FLOUR

3 TABLESPOONS BROWN SUGAR

Cover vegetables with salt and let stand for 24 hours. Drain. Mix together mustard, ginger, turmeric, flour, and sugar. Blend to a smooth paste with a little of the vinegar. Bring the remaining vinegar to a boil. Pour over paste, stirring well, then return to the pan. Bring to a boil and cook for 3 minutes, stirring carefully.

Add vegetables and simmer gently for 10 minutes. Cool slightly, then pour into clean, warm jars. Cover with lids and screw caps.

YIELD: 3½ PINTS

Corn Relish

9 MEDIUM EARS CORN

1 QUART CIDER VINEGAR

1 CUP SUGAR

1 TABLESPOON SALT

1½ TABLESPOONS DRY MUSTARD

1 TEASPOON TURMERIC

1 SMALL CABBAGE,
CHOPPED

2 MEDIUM WHITE ONIONS,
CHOPPED

3 RED PEPPERS,
SEEDED AND CHOPPED

2 GREEN PEPPERS,
SEEDED AND CHOPPED

Cook corn in boiling water for 2 minutes. Rinse in cold water. Cut or scrape corn from cob.

Mix together vinegar, sugar, salt, and spices. Bring to a boil and add vegetables. Boil about 30 minutes, or until vegetables are tender, stirring constantly. Pour into clean hot jars and seal.

YIELD: 8 PINTS

Beet Chutney

Especially nice with pork chops or roasts. Rub ½ lemon on your hands to remove stains.

3 POUNDS RED BEETS

1½ POUNDS COOKING APPLES,
PEELED AND CHOPPED

2 ONIONS

1 PINT DARK VINEGAR

1 CUP SUGAR

6 CLOVES

Cook beets until tender, then cut into cubes. Place apples, onions, vinegar, sugar, and cloves in a large enamel pot. Cook for 30 minutes over low heat, stirring often. Add beets and cook 15 minutes. Pour into hot clean jars and seal.

YIELD: 5 OR 6 EIGHT-OUNCE JARS

English Pickled Onions

This is my mother's recipe. It keeps well and tastes terrific. Small onions are easiest to get into jars, but I use all sizes.

4 QUARTS MALT VINEGAR

20 POUND ONIONS,
PEELED

PICKLING SPICES IN MUSLIN BAGS
(2 TEASPOONS FOR QUART JARS,
1 TEASPOON FOR PINTS)

Sterilize the jars. Bring malt vinegar to the boil. The canning bath should be boiling and ready.

Put 2 or 3 onions into each jar, then add the appropriate spice bag. Fill each jar with onions, then cover with the boiling malt vinegar. Seal and process in the boiling bath for 20 minutes.

YIELD: ABOUT 10 QUART JARS

Dilled Cucumbers

Do not used waxed cucumbers. Buy 3- to 4-inch cucumbers and scrub thoroughly.

Fill each sterilized jar with cucumbers, leaving 1 inch at the top. For each quart, add 1 teaspoon mustard seed and 1 or 2 sprigs of fresh dill. Keep warm.

Prepare the brine: For each quart, boil 1 cup white vinegar, 2 cups water, and 1 tablespoon salt. Pour over cucumbers to within ½-inch of the top. Seal and process in boiling water bath for 20 minutes, timing from the immersion of jars into the canner. Remove from water bath and store in a cool place.

Dilled Green Tomatoes

We pick any green tomatoes remaining on the vines just before the first frost comes along to blacken them.

Wash tomatoes in cold water and drain. Sort out the smallest ones, do the same with the medium-sized tomatoes, and the largest ones. Cut the large tomatoes in half. Process all three sizes in separate batches. Proceed as in the recipe for dilled cucumbers.

Canned Tomatoes

Skin ½ bushel of firm ripe tomatoes by dipping each tomato into boiling water for 1 minute.

Place tomatoes in a large pot and bring to a boil. No water is necessary because tomatoes make juice very quickly. Stir the pot once or twice.

Fill the canning kettle with water and bring to a boil.

Prepare 7 or 8 quart jars and lids: Wash in soapy water, rinse well, then fill with warm water.

When tomatoes are boiling, remove from heat. Empty each jar of warm water and fill with hot tomatoes to within 1 inch of top. Add 1 tablespoon fresh lemon juice and 1 teaspoon salt to each jar. Seal and proceed until all jars are filled. Process in the canning kettle for 20 minutes, timing from the immersion of the jars into the water. Cool and store.

Pickled Walnuts

Use slightly unripe walnuts. Prick with a fork in several places, then soak in a brine of 2 tablespoons salt for every pint of cold water for 3 days.

Drain and arrange on a tray or cloth. Set in the sun for 1 to 3 days, turning nuts from time to time. The walnuts will turn black.

When black, pack the nuts into jars and fill with spiced malt or cider vinegar to within ½-inch of the top. Age 1 month before using.

Notes

Culinary Postscript

My song should be "Come day, go day, God send the weekends." We are fortunate to get away for weekends in Cheshire, Connecticut where we have nearly 30 acres of beautiful country. We grow all the vegetables we can take care of at the farm. My son, Peter, is in charge of the crops because he is the one who insisted on buying a big tiller to make the work easier. He was right—the tiller does a job-and-a-half turning over the soil. How well I remember the blisters from the hand digging we did the first years. But our rewards were great. To be able to pick our own vegetables or salad makings is marvelous. What a terrific coincidence that I was born and raised in the county of Cheshire in old England and that our farm today is in Cheshire, New England. Connecticut has many towns named after places in England and the countryside is so similar that I don't feel too far away. I have the rose garden and big mint bed that are prerequisites in England.

In Connecticut we have big, beautiful tomatoes growing abundantly. In England most tomatoes are grown in glasshouses. My Mam would go daft if she saw how many tomatoes we have on the farm. I remember coming as a bride to my in-laws' farm in Meriden, Connecticut. There before my eyes were rows and rows of tomatoes and green peppers, which I though were green tomatoes, not having seen a green pepper before. What a pleasure to pick a tomato, wipe it off with the palm of my hand, and eat it. We were short of everything during World War II and I looked at a tomato with great appreciation before eating it.

Well, on with the present. On our property we have chokecherries, elderber-ries, wild grapes, blackberries, black walnut and apple trees. We gather princess fern at Christmas time to decorate Country Host and my home.

My two grandsons especially love haying time. We have a nearby farmer who cuts and bales the hay from about 8 acres of our land. We keep 30 bales of hay for mulching the vegetable garden, the strawberry patch, and my rose garden. When the grass is high, the little ones and I play hide-and-seek. The grass just hides them and if they were not so blond, I would never find them.

Country air makes everyone very hungry and we love to pack a bag full of Country Host pies before leaving for Connecticut. Sausage rolls, meat pies, and cheeses usually constitute our evening meal—or a snack in between times. My grandsons and I get up fairly early on the weekends. When the early morning sunshine brings the birds out and the big crows start cawing we get ready for the long, full summer day. The boys and I have breakfast in the screen house. I make pancakes with maple syrup, a big pot of tea for me, and coffee for the rest of the family. The little ones like cambric tea made with lots of milk and just a dash of tea. If the morning is damp I fry bacon, eggs, sausage, tomatoes, and bread fried in the liquid left after frying the tomatoes. This is solidly English food. A good friend who is a chef in the lake district comes to the United States often and has access to the best foods in this country. But when he visits us, it is what he invariably requests.

When breakfast is over we all have work to do. Peter and his wife, Linda, go to the garden, while my son Christopher and whoever else is with us for the weekend are on the lawn-mowing detail. The little ones and I look for berries. I am the cook for every meal— we all do the job we do best.

When the rhubarb is ready, my grandsons cut the leaves off the rhubarb stalks. We have a mulch pit where we toss all the grass cuttings and leaves— it gives us very rich soil. When we first acquired the farm, we did not have too many birds around. Now the birds get the stale bread and rolls from the shop. The food attracts robins, blue jays, cardinals, and yellow finches. They seem to stay away from the strawberries and raspberries when we put out the bread.

On weekends when we have visitors I usually make a different menu fit for a country visitor. I bring a big smoked ham from the shop, score the top fat in a diamond design, stick cloves into the cuts, and sprinkle with brown sugar. Then I put the ham into a deep roasting pan, add 1 quart water, and bake it for 3 hours in a 325°F. oven. After it cools, I decorate the top with pineapple and orange slices or fresh parsley. Potato and zucchini salads, slices of black pumpernickel bread, sweet butter, and a pot of good mustard are placed on the table. For a really special treat I make raisin scones. A slice of ham on a raisin scone is terrific. When tomatoes are ripe, I slice a huge amount into a bowl, add a couple of crushed oregano leaves from my herb garden, a twist of black pepper, and there you are. We drink cider. For dessert I make lemon meringue pie and a big moist chocolate cake to serve with tea and coffee, or sometimes just bring out a chunk of Cheshire cheese and crackers. Simple as

this food sounds the table always looks inviting. With the colorful ham and fresh green salads, the rosy tomatoes, the raisin-studded scones, the black bread, a bowl of apples and some wildflowers serving as center pieces, my old oak dining table seems to glow with contentment.

Time passes quickly when there's a lot to do. We frequently weed the garden and pick wildflowers and the ripe fruits and vegetables for our return to the city. Sometimes we have such a bounty to bring back in the car that there's hardly enough room for us and my son's cocker spaniel!

During the apple season, I can't wait to get home and make cakes, chutneys, and pies. Strawberry time is another busy time for me. Have you ever smelled 50 quarts of strawberries enclosed in a car? It's just unbelievable, and we always reach the city minus a basket or two. The next day I make the strawberry jam.

We buy big brown eggs from a neighboring farmer, to use in baking and to sell over the counter. Fresh country eggs remind me of my childhood and of the Rhode Island Reds we kept in England. My sister and I had a special hen named Doris who laid one big brown speckled egg every day.

Apples

Apples are worthwhile to freeze if you can get a good buy on them during the peak season.

Peel, core, and slice apples and divide them into quart amounts. Immerse sliced apples in 1 gallon of water with 1 tablespoon of salt for 15 minutes. Drain, then add half a cup of sugar for each quart of apples. Mix, put into plastic bags and freeze immediately.

Applesauce

Traditional accompaniment for goose or duck.

6 TART APPLES,
PEELED, CORED, AND SLICED

½ CUP WATER

2 TABLESPOONS SWEET BUTTER

1 TABLESPOON BROWN SUGAR

4 CLOVES

Put apples and water into a pan. Add butter, brown sugar, and cloves. Cover and cook for 20 minutes over a medium low heat, or until apples are tender. Puree apples through a food mill or in a blender. Return to pan and cook gently for 15 to 20 minutes. Cool to room temperature before serving.

6 TO 8 SERVINGS

Mulled Cider

1 QUART CIDER

¾ CUP SUGAR

15 CLOVES

6 STICKS CINNAMON

12 WHOLE ALLSPICE

Heat all of the ingredients until sugar dissolves—do not boil. Pour through a strainer to remove the spices. Serve hot.

6 TO 8 SERVINGS

Cider Syllabub

1 CUP PASTURIZED HEAVY CREAM

RIND AND JUICE OF ½ LEMON

3 TABLESPOONS SUGAR

¼ CUP CIDER

Whip cream until thick but not stiff. Mix in rind, lemon juice, and sugar. Gradually blend in cider. Pile into 4 dessert glasses and refrigerate.

4 SERVINGS

Beef Drippings

Beef drippings can be made from the suet of beef kidneys and steak trimmings. Cut fat into cubes and place over slow heat in a heavy steel pot, stirring occasionally until cubes are dark brown. Cool, then press fat through sieve. Store in containers in the refrigerator.

Sprinkle salt on the cracklings and eat as you would nuts. A few cracklings tossed into mashed potatoes are marvelous.

Drippings are delicious used on toast instead of butter. It is especially soothing for a sore throat.

Suggestions for the Use of Stale Bread

Croutons for Soups or Salads

Cut stale bread into slices about 1/3-inch thick. Remove all crust and spread with butter. Cut into medium cubes and bake in a 350°F. oven until lightly browned. Store in plastic bags in the refrigerator until needed.

Cheese Sticks

Cut stale bread into long narrow strips. Spread generously with butter, then thickly coat with grated cheddar cheese. Place in a 350°F. oven until brown. These are delicious with soup.

Browned Bread Crumbs

Make 8 slices of stale bread into crumbs. Melt 8 tablespoons butter in a frying pan. Brown the butter, being careful not to burn it. Add bread crumbs to butter, stirring constantly until crumbs are browned. Serve hot as garnish for cooked vegetables.

Clarified Butter

Melt ½ pound butter until a clear golden liquid appears. A creamy sediment will form on the bottom of the pan. Strain the clear liquid through cheesecloth. Refrigerate.

A Few Thoughts on English Cheshire Cheese

The county of Cheshire is the heart of the farmhouse Cheshire cheese industry. Generations of farm families have carried on the tradition of making cheese during the summer months when cows produce more milk than the family can drink.

My Grandad Peters wanted me to learn cheese-making and I was always hanging around the dairy, more interested in watching the milk flow over the pasturizer than in how to make curds and whey. A few years ago I made up for that inattention by watching my Uncle Tom make cheese in the same dairy. The process is just about the same as it was centuries ago. He produced the red and white Cheshire cheeses as well as the rare Cheshire blue cheese. Only 5 or 6 wheels out of every 100 cheeses are turned to sweet-flavored blues.

One gallon of milk produces one pound of cheese. Thousands of gallons of milk are kept in storage tanks. The milk is pumped into a stainless steel vat where a bacteria culture is added to sour the milk and start it working. The milk is heated and rennet is added to clot the milk and make curds and whey. The whey is drained off and given to pigs as a food supplement. The curds are broken up and chopped to resemble fine bread crumbs. Salt is added to the curds, then they are put into molds and pressed for 24 hours.

After the cheeses are turned out of the molds they are wrapped, waxed, and stored for about 3 weeks. The cheese can be eaten after this time, but it develops a better flavor as it ages. Blues are wrapped in cheesecloth that is larded and floured.

The rare Cheshire blue cheese was an accident of nature and in the old days cheese makers regarded the cheese as unfit to eat. Farm wives' tales claim it is good to heal cuts—rub a cut with a piece of Cheshire blue cheese and the cut would heal.

Fritter Batter

This batter can be used for sweet or savory fritters. Thin slices of zucchini, eggplant, cauliflowerets, onion rings, and potatoes are excellent when covered with batter and deep fried.

1½ CUPS OF ALL-PURPOSE FLOUR

¼ TEASPOON SALT

2 TEASPOONS BAKING POWDER

1 EGG,
WELL BEATEN

2/3 CUPS MILK

2 TABLESPOONS CONFECTIONER'S
SUGAR (OMIT FOR SAVORY FRITTERS)

Sift dry ingredients together. Add egg and milk. Mix to a stiff batter. The batter should be thick enough to coat whatever is being fried. If too thick, add a little more milk; if too thin, add a little more flour. Let batter rest for at least 1 hour before using.

Icings

To use both almond paste and marzipan, roll out like pastry between 2 pieces of plastic wrap, remove top piece of plastic and invert paste onto the cake.

Almond Paste

12 OUNCES FINE SEMOLINA

16 OUNCES SUPERFINE GRANULATED SUGAR

3 TEASPOONS ALMOND EXTRACT

COLD WATER

3 EGG YOLKS

Mix semolina and sugar. Combine almond extract and a little cold water with egg yolks. Beat well. Gradually add egg mixture to the dry ingredients. Do not make mixture too wet. Knead the paste until smooth. Keep in a covered bowl until ready to use.

ENOUGH FOR A LARGE CAKE

Marzipan

1¼ POUND ALMONDS,
GROUND

10 OUNCES CONFECTIONER'S SUGAR,
SIFTED

10 OUNCES SUPERFINE GRANULATED
SUGAR

½ TEASPOON ALMOND EXTRACT

1½ TEASPOON VANILLA EXTRACT

1½ TEASPOON ROSE WATER

JUICE OF 1 LEMON

1 EGG WHITE,
BEATEN

Mix almonds and the two sugars together. Add lemon juice, almond and vanilla extract, and rose water. Add enough of the egg white to make a dry soft paste. Quickly knead all ingredients to a smooth paste. Do not overwork paste because it will become oily. If paste is too wet, add more ground almonds. If too dry, add a little more rose water. Keep covered in a cool place until ready to use.

ENOUGH FOR A LARGE CAKE

Royal Icing

8 CUPS CONFECTIONER'S SUGAR,
SIFTED

5 EGG WHITES

¼ TEASPOON SALT

1 TEASPOON LEMON JUICE

1 TABLESPOON GLYCERINE

¼ TEASPOON CREAM OF TARTAR

Beat egg whites with 3 or 4 tablespoons of sugar. When egg whites begin to stiffen, slowly add the remaining sugar, salt, lemon juice, glycerine, and cream of tartar. Mix until all sugar is used and a very white icing appears. (My mum used to add a drop of Reckitt's Laundry Bluing to the icing at the end to get that stark white appearance.)

Carefully scrape any icing from the sides of the bowl. Cover with a piece of plastic wrap or a folded cloth. This icing hardens quickly.

When ready to use, apply icing to cake with a metal spatula. Dip spatula into hot water. Smooth icing on top and sides of cake as though plastering a wall. Spread icing on roughly at first, then smooth with the wetted spatula.

ENOUGH FOR A LARGE CAKE

Chocolate Butter Icing

8 OUNCES SWEET BUTTER,
SOFTENED

3½ TO 4 CUPS CONFECTIONER'S SUGAR

6 TABLESPOONS DARK COCOA
(DROSTÉ IS BEST)

2 TEASPOONS VANILLA EXTRACT

Cream butter and confectioner's sugar. Blend in cocoa, mixing well. Turn into electric mixer, add vanilla and mix at high speed until smooth, about 5 minutes. Spread top and sides of cake with icing.

ENOUGH FOR A 9-INCH LAYER CAKE

Mama's Chocolate Frosting

4 SQUARES UNSWEETENED
CHOCOLATE,
GRATED

2 TABLESPOONS HOT WATER

1 CUP CONFECTIONER'S SUGAR,
SIFTED

2 EGGS,
WELL BEATEN

½ CUP UNSALTED BUTTER

Melt chocolate in double boiler. Add hot water and mix well. Remove from heat. Leave mixture over hot water in double boiler and add eggs and sugar. Stir for 2 or 3 minutes, or until mixture is slightly thickened. Add butter a little at a time, blending after each addition. Transfer frosting to a bowl and cool. This frosting keeps well in the refrigerator.

ENOUGH FOR AN 8-INCH LAYER CAKE

Pastry

I have always enjoyed making pastry. The feel of the flour running through my fingers is cooling. Very often when I have thinking to do, I make pastry. Successful pastry making comes with practice—there are several do's and don'ts that I have learned through trial and error. It is better to use all-purpose flour for all pastry. The quicker the fat is worked into the flour, the better. Always sift flour before using—this lightens the pastry. Use a large bowl for the pastry ingredients because more air gets to the flour. Always keep ingredients, the bowl, and your hands as cool as possible. Pastry should be rolled one way—away from you—and turned to the right to get the desired shape.

The consistency of the pastry is important. Pastry that is too wet becomes hard when baked. Too dry and the dough will not roll out. I find the texture to be just right when the pastry rolls into a ball with very little handling. I favor butter or lard for pastry most of the time, but there are other fats that can be used, such as suet, margarine, and oil.

Pastry should be baked at 400° or 425°F. The one exception is for apple pies. I bake them in a moderate 350°F. oven because the slower cooking produces a better pie filling when fresh apples are used. The crust is always good.

Puff pastry is quite a production, but worth the effort for some of the dreamy desserts that can be made with it as well as vol-au-vent cases for all kinds of fillings. Flan pastry for sweet tarts is marvelous and easy to use.

Other recipes included here with a few of their possible uses are: *choux pastry* for cream puffs or eclairs; *flaky pastry* for sausage rolls and mince pies; *raised pastry* for veal and ham pies; *hot water crust pastry* for cold pork pies and hot meat pies; *potato pastry* for meat pies or casseroles; *suet crust pastry* for savory or sweet puddings; and *cream cheese pastry.*

I have several rolling pins of differing sizes—regular and ball-bearing types. I use the rolling pins every day—or so it seems—and would be lost without them.

Regular Shortcrust Pastry

2 CUPS ALL-PURPOSE FLOUR

¼ TEASPOON SALT

4 TABLESPOONS BUTTER

4 TABLESPOONS LARD

2 TO 3 TABLESPOONS COLD WATER

Sift flour and salt together. Quickly cut in butter and lard with finger tips until mixture looks like bread crumbs. Gradually add enough water to make a firm dough of rolling consistency.

NOTE: Instead of butter and lard, 8 tablespoons of vegetable or corn oil can be used. Mix into the flour and salt, then add enough water to make dough. When oil is used, the pastry should be rolled out very quickly because the oil tends to settle in the bottom of the pastry bowl if allowed to stand. Place the oil pastry between 2 sheets of plastic wrap or wax paper to roll it out.

YIELD: 2 CRUSTS FOR ONE 9-INCH PIE

Sweet Shortcrust Pastry

Add 1½ tablespoons of sugar to ingredients listed for *Regular Shortcrust Pastry,* and omit the salt. Cream sugar and fat together, then mix in flour and enough water to make a firm dough.

YIELD: 2 CRUSTS FOR ONE 9-INCH PIE

Crispy Shortcrust Pastry

4 CUPS ALL-PURPOSE FLOUR

1 TEASPOON SALT

1 CUP VEGETABLE OIL

½ CUP COLD WATER

Sift flour and salt. Mix in oil. Add water and mix to a stiff dough. Cut dough into 4 pieces. Roll out one piece at a time between 2 pieces of plastic wrap to 1/8-inch thickness. Cut into 3½-inch circles. Press each circle into tartlet tins. Prick all over with a fork and bake in a 375°F. oven for 15 to 20 minutes until golden brown. These tartlet shells can be made in quantity and kept wrapped in foil in a cool place. Fill with jam or curd for a pretty tray of sweets.

YIELD: 50 TARTLETS

Puff Pastry

2 CUPS ALL-PURPOSE FLOUR

16 TABLESPOONS SWEET BUTTER

¼ TEASPOON SALT

2 TO 3 TABLESPOONS COLD WATER

SQUEEZE OF LEMON JUICE

Sift flour and salt together onto pastry board. Mix to a rolling consistency with cold water and lemon juice. Roll to oblong shape. Shape butter into a block. Place block of butter in center of pastry. Fold bottom section of pastry over butter then fold top section down so that butter is completely covered. Turn the dough at right angles and seal edges. Using the rolling pin, press across dough to distribute the butter and air somewhat. Carefully roll out. Flour the rolling pin when necessary. Fold dough into envelope as before, turn it, seal edges, pound lightly, and roll out again. Repeat this five times, making seven rollings in all. If the pastry becomes sticky and soft, put the dough in the refrigerator to firm up. Rest the dough in the refrigerator before the final rolling and again before baking. Bake in a 475°F. oven for the first 10 to 15 minutes, then lower to 400°F. and bake until golden, about 10 minutes. The higher heat at the beginning makes the dough rise and keeps the butter in. Good puff pastry should rise 4 or 5 times the original thickness.

Flan Pastry

8 TABLESPOONS SWEET BUTTER

1½ TABLESPOONS SUGAR

2 CUPS ALL-PURPOSE FLOUR

¼ TEASPOON SALT

2 TO 3 TABLESPOONS COLD WATER

Cream butter and sugar until light and creamy. Sift flour and salt together and add to creamed butter. Mix with knife or spoon, gradually adding enough water to make a firm rolling consistency. Roll pastry into a ball. If preparing flan shells, bake blind in a 425°F. oven until lightly browned.

NOTE: Baking blind is a partial baking of an empty shell. To prevent pastry from rising, place a piece of wax paper on the bottom of shell and cover with raw rice or beans or another pie pan. Remove paper and filling 5 minutes before shell finishes cooking to brown.

Choux Pastry

3 OUNCES ALL-PURPOSE FLOUR

½ CUP WATER

1/8 TEASPOON SUGAR

2 TABLESPOONS BUTTER

2 WHOLE EGGS PLUS 1 YOLK, WELL BEATEN

In a heavy saucepan, gently melt the butter with water and sugar. Stir in flour. Cook over low heat, stirring constantly until mixture forms a ball and leaves the sides of the pan clean.

Remove pan from heat and gradually add 1 egg at a time, beating until incorporated. Cool mixture. Use for cream puffs or eclairs.

Force the mixture through a pastry bag into walnut-sized mounds onto a lightly greased baking sheet. Bake in a 375°F. oven until golden brown. These tiny puffs can be filled with whipped cream and served with chocolate sauce. Other sizes can be formed for cream puffs or eclairs.

Flaky Pastry

2 CUPS ALL-PURPOSE FLOUR

¼ TEASPOON SALT

¾ CUP (6 OUNCES) BUTTER

3 TO 4 TABLESPOONS COLD WATER

Sift flour with salt. Divide butter into 3 pieces. Rub flour and 1/3 of the butter together until mixture resembles bread crumbs. Add just enough water to hold ingredients together. On a lightly floured board, roll out to an oblong shape. Chop the next piece of butter into small pieces and place the pieces on 2/3 of the dough. Leave remaining 1/3 of dough without butter. Take the corners of the unbuttered pastry and fold it over half of buttered side. Take the open piece and fold over on top of the last fold—just like closing an envelope. Turn pastry at right angles, seal open ends and lightly pound the pastry to evenly distribute the butter. Roll into an oblong shape. Repeat this procedure with the remaining butter. Refrigerate pastry for 30 minutes to rest. Fold and roll the pastry 3 more times. Refrigerate for 30 minutes before using. Bake at 475°F. heat for 15 minutes, then lower heat to 400°F. and bake until golden.

Raised Pastry

3 CUPS ALL-PURPOSE FLOUR

½ TEASPOON SALT

8 TABLESPOONS VEGETABLE SHORTENING OR LARD

½ CUP WARM WATER

Sift flour and salt together. Melt fat in water and add to flour. Mix with your fingers to a consistency that is easy to roll out. Keep warm until ready to use.

Hot Water Crust Pastry

This might seem to be a lot, but it is just right for a family-sized meat pie. The quantities can be halved and used for two smaller pies.

14 CUPS ALL-PURPOSE FLOUR

1 POUND LARD

1 PINT WATER

½ TEASPOON SALT

Heat flour in 300°F. oven until hot. Boil lard, water, and salt. Pour over flour and mix with a wooden spoon. When cool enough to handle, turn onto a lightly floured board. Knead for 15 minutes. Roll out. This pastry should be baked in a 425°F. oven for 30 minutes, then in a 400°F. oven to finish cooking time.

Potato Pastry

This pastry is very good for meat turnovers and for topping casserole dishes.

4 OUNCES MASHED POTATOES

1 CUP ALL-PURPOSE FLOUR

8 TABLESPOONS LARD

½ TEASPOON SALT

1½ TO 2 TABLESPOONS COLD WATER

Sift flour and salt. Rub in lard. Add potatoes and mix. Turn onto a lightly floured board and knead well. Add enough water to make firm consistency. Bake in a 350°F. oven—45 minutes for turnovers and 40 minutes for casseroles.

Suet Crust Pastry

For steamed or boiled puddings—sweet and savory.

2 CUPS ALL-PURPOSE FLOUR

2 TEASPOONS BAKING POWDER

1/8 TEASPOON SALT

4 OUNCES BEEF SUET,
GRATED

3 TO 4 TABLESPOONS COLD WATER

Sift flour, baking powder, and salt. Add suet. Mix to a rolling consistency with cold water. Roll out thinly because this pastry rises. Line a 2-pint pudding bowl with the pastry. Add the filling, then roll out a top to cover the bowl. Cover with wax paper and tie down under lip of bowl. Cover with a pudding cloth. Steam or boil rapidly with lid on pot for 2½ to 3 hours, depending on filling. Fruit takes less cooking time than meat. Be sure water is always boiling and replenish water as needed.

Cream Cheese Pastry

Mama always made these little Hungarian pastries called *Kifli* for special holidays.

3 CUPS FLOUR

8 OUNCES CREAM CHEESE

1 CUP BUTTER

CONFECTIONER'S SUGAR

Thoroughly mix cream cheese and butter into flour. Collect into a ball. Pinch off dough into 50 balls. Refrigerate overnight. Roll out each ball to a 4-inch circle on a board covered with confectioner's sugar. Fill each circle with nut or jam filling of your choice. Bake for 20 to 25 minutes in a 350°F. oven.

Salad Dressings

Italian

½ CUP VEGETABLE OIL

2 TABLESPOONS LEMON JUICE

2 TABLESPOONS VINEGAR

½ TEASPOON SALT

PEPPER,
FRESHLY GROUND

½ TEASPOON OREGANO

1 CLOVE GARLIC,
MINCED (OPTIONAL)

Combine all of the ingredients, mixing well.

French

To the ingredients listed above, add a pinch of tarragon and ½ teaspoon lemon zest. Omit the garlic.

Stocks

Beef

Brown 5 pounds of beef soup bones (available from butchers) in a roasting pot in a 350°F. oven for 1 hour. Add ¼ cup water to prevent sticking. Remove bones from oven and place in a large soup pot. Cover the bones with 5 quarts of water, bring to a boil, cover and simmer for 2½ hours. Strain and cool before storing.

Chicken

Save a good supply of chicken bones. Keep them frozen until you are ready to use.

In a large stock pot, cover at least 5 pounds of chicken bones with cold water. Bring to a boil and simmer for about 2½ hours. Strain the liquid and let it cool. Store in the refrigerator or freezer.

This stock is used as a base for sauces and soups or as a flavorful liquid for cooking rice and vegetables. It is best to add seasoning when preparing the final dish.

Index